Jump Start
Your Career in Library
and Information Science

Jump Start
Your Career in Library
and Information Science

Priscilla K. Shontz

with the assistance of Steven J. Oberg

Illustrations by Robert N. Klob

The Scarecrow Press, Inc.
Lanham, Maryland, and London
2002

SCARECROW PRESS, INC.

Published in the United States of America
by Scarecrow Press, Inc.
4720 Boston Way
Lanham, Maryland 20706
www.scarecrowpress.com

4 Pleydell Gardens, Folkestone
Kent CT20 2DN, England

British Library Cataloguing-in-Publication Information Available

Library of Congress Cataloging-in-Publication Data

Shontz, Priscilla K., 1965–
    Jump start your career in library and information science / Priscilla K. Shontz, with the
assistance of Steven J. Oberg ; illustrations by Robert N. Klob.
        p. cm.
    Includes bibliographical references.
    ISBN 0-8108-4084-7 (alk. paper)
        1. Library science—Vocational guidance. 2. Information science—Vocational guidance.
    3. Librarians—Employment. 4. Librarians—Interviews. 5. Career development. I. Oberg,
    Steven J. II. Title.

Z682.35.V62 S47 2002
020'.23—dc21

                                                                                    2001049614

∞™ The paper used in this publication meets the minimum requirements of American
National Standard for Information Sciences—Permanence of Paper for Printed Library
Materials, ANSI/NISO Z39.48-1992.
Manufactured in the United States of America.

In loving memory of Kay L. Dorn, 1934–2001

Contents

Tables

Foreword

I wish this book had been available when I was starting out in my library career. Priscilla Shontz's *Jump Start Your Career in Library and Information Science* is the essential "owner's manual" for building a successful career in library science—or any other field, for that matter. This is the definitive source to consult for information on career planning, job searching, networking, mentoring, and leadership skills, among others. Successful and rewarding careers don't just happen, and Shontz's book clearly outlines the range of areas and strategies needed to build the career you want.

Several things set Shontz's book apart from other career guides. One of these is the selection of firsthand accounts from dozens of librarians she interviewed over a two-year period. Especially useful are the "day in the life of" accounts in the chapter on career planning. Here, a diverse group of librarians, ranging from reference and school librarians to those in more nontraditional careers, such as systems and sales, describe in their own words what it takes to succeed in their chosen area of librarianship. Particularly helpful are the chapters devoted to succeeding in the workplace. The chapter on interpersonal skills, for example, details key strategies for working effectively with supervisors and coworkers. Shontz devotes considerable attention to networking and the importance of involvement in professional associations. Each chapter concludes with an excellent list of sources, including Web sites, for further reading.

Shontz brings considerable expertise to this topic. Through her work with the American Library Association and its New Members Round Table, she has devoted a significant amount of her professional life to helping new librarians develop career skills. While Shontz's book should be required reading for every library school student, it also provides a wealth of valuable information for all librarians regardless of where they are on the career ladder. Though specifically tailored for the library community, those in other fields will find the practical tips and advice offered

here to be invaluable. This is one source that librarians will turn to again
and again throughout their careers.

Robert R. Newlen

Head, Legislative Relations Office
Congressional Research Service
Library of Congress

Preface

This book is designed to help new librarians begin to manage a successful and satisfying career in the library and information science profession. The first years of a librarian's career are often overwhelming, and yet these years can be the key to creating a successful career. Masters of Library Science (MLS) students and new information professionals need guidance and support in order to make the most of their careers. Unless one is fortunate enough to have good mentors or strong support groups, a new librarian may drift into an unsatisfying career. This book emphasizes the value of defining one's own idea of success and of positioning oneself to be prepared to take advantage of opportunities that arise. Although the book is aimed at students and new information professionals, much of the advice may apply to a librarian at any stage of his or her career.

The advice compiled in this book was gathered from library and nonlibrary literature, questionnaires, presentations, e-mail messages, discussion lists, interviews, and conversations with more than seventy information professionals over a two-year period. The book quotes advice directly as much as possible, so that the reader can "hear" the advice and anecdotes in the contributor's own words. Please note that a person's job title and institution are listed only the first time that the person is quoted in the book.

The book is written in a practical, easy-to-read style so that a busy reader may pick the book up and read a short section whenever he or she has time. It is written in a modular format so that the reader can read any chapter independently of other chapters. The book is organized into eight broad topics: career planning, job searching, experience and education, interpersonal skills, networking, leadership skills, mentoring, and writing for publication. Because the book covers such a wide variety of topics, it cannot go into detail about any one subject. Lengthy lists of related readings, as well as related Web sites, are included to allow the reader to follow up on any topic.

In writing this book, I have drawn on my own experience as a new librarian and on the advice I have gathered from mentors, colleagues, friends, and professors throughout my career so far. I have been extremely inspired by my interactions with others in the library field, particularly new librarians, students, and others who are genuinely excited about contributing to our profession. I have learned a great deal while writing this book, and I hope this book offers helpful advice for your career.

Acknowledgments

Steve Oberg played a key role in this project. Although numerous major life changes prevented him from cowriting the book as we'd planned, he read articles, gathered information from contacts and friends, and shared ideas and suggestions. Thank you so much, Steve, for your interest in and valuable contribution to this project.

Robert Newlen and Ann Snoeyenbos inspired this book. Robert's helpful, practical résumé book made me think about related career books I'd like to see. The phrase "jump start your career," jotted down on a piece of paper in Ann's ALA NMRT president files, inspired the book's title and theme. Robert commented on my book proposal, read drafts, and graciously wrote the book's foreword. Ann listened to my ideas and offered her own unique perspectives, advice, and encouragement. Thank you, Robert and Ann.

Wayne Jones has been amazingly generous with his time and expertise, reading drafts, offering very helpful suggestions, and encouraging me along the way. I truly couldn't have done this without you, Wayne.

I'd like to thank Jose Gonzalez and the Texas A&M University Corpus Christi Bell Library Interlibrary Loan department for getting me many, many articles and books from other libraries.

I'd also like to thank Bea Caraway, Nancy Cunningham, Jill Emery, Beverley Geer, and Rachel Singer Gordon for listening to me and encouraging me. Writing this book was much more difficult than I'd anticipated, and these friends kept me going when I felt overwhelmed.

Thank you to everyone who responded to our questions and offered such useful advice and interesting anecdotes. I'd particularly like to thank NMRT-L and NEWLIB-L discussion list subscribers who offered interesting questions and perspectives.

A special thanks goes to my father, Robert Klob, for drawing the illustrations for this book. It's very special to have him be part of this project.

I couldn't have finished this project without the encouragement, support, patience, and love of my husband. He not only provided ideas for the book and advice for managing the project but he buoyed me up when I was ready to quit. Thank you, David, for everything.

Introduction

What do I want to do "when I grow up?" What is my ideal job? How do I get there?

Have you ever asked yourself these questions? Most of us will ask ourselves these questions over and over throughout our professional lives, and our answers will probably change from year to year.

The goal of this book is to help you define what you enjoy and help you begin to manage a career that satisfies you. Success differs for each of us. It is not necessarily directing a large library system, publishing numerous books, holding a high-profile position in a professional association, or making a lot of money. What do you enjoy doing? What tasks or environments do you find satisfying, challenging, inspiring, interesting, or rewarding? Perhaps you want to direct a large academic library. Perhaps you want a job that allows you to spend a great deal of time with your family or outside interests. Perhaps you want to try a new type of work every few years. Perhaps you want a job that offers stability or opportunities for internal advancement. Do you crave stimulation? Stability? Public contact? What makes you happy? In order to create a satisfying career, you must first define your own idea of success.

This book is organized into eight broad topics: career planning, job searching, experience and education, interpersonal skills, networking, leadership skills, mentoring, and writing for publication. The book is designed so that you can read any chapter on its own or read the chapters in any order, choosing which chapters are most relevant to you at any point in your career.

In chapter 1, I discuss career planning. This chapter describes some methods for assessing your goals, your skills, and the job market as you try to determine what type of jobs interest you. Chapter 2 introduces job searching techniques, including writing a résumé, interviewing, and negotiating a job offer. Chapter 3 covers practical strategies for getting varied experience and education in the first few years of your career. Chapter 4 shares how personal and professional networks can help you further your career, broaden your perspective on your profession, and even develop friendships. Chapter 5 examines techniques for developing social and communication skills, as well as strategies for dealing with different personality types and difficult coworkers and supervisors. Chapter 6 discusses mentoring and being mentored. Chapter 7 addresses learning to lead even when not in a supervisory role. This chapter also shares advice for new supervisors. In chapter 8, I discuss strategies for those beginning to write and publish. In conclusion, chapter 9 reminds us to be open to opportunity while learning what we find satisfying.

A large number of information professionals contributed advice for this book. I have learned a great deal while gathering advice from successful people in our field. I hope this book is useful to others who are in the early stages of a career in library and information science. You may find all the advice a bit overwhelming. Don't feel you have to agree with all the advice—or even read it all at one time! I hope you will use the advice in this book to help you determine what you want from your career, and to position yourself to take advantage of opportunities that come your way.

CHAPTER 1

Career Planning

"Where were you last night?"
"That's so long ago, I don't remember."
"Will I see you tonight?"
"I never make plans that far in advance."

—conversation between Yvonne and Rick Blaine, *Casablanca* (1942)

I don't want to sell anything, buy anything, or process anything as a career. I don't want to sell anything bought or processed, or buy anything sold or processed, or process anything sold, bought, or processed, or repair anything sold, bought, or processed. You know, as a career, I don't want to do that.

—Lloyd Dobler, *Say Anything* (1989)

Have you ever been asked in an interview, "Where do you see yourself in five years?" or "Describe your ideal job." How would you answer those questions? Although it is important to stay flexible, it is also essential to think about your career, your strengths, and your interests when deciding what type of job or career best fits you. Career planning begins with self-assessment. Before planning your ideal career path, spend time assessing your own interests, talents, skills, goals, and limitations. Assess the job market. What jobs best utilize the skills you have? Which jobs use the skills you most enjoy using? Develop a skills improvement plan. What skills would you need to learn to get your dream job? What skills can you learn that will help you on any job? Assessing your own goals, interests, and skills better prepares you to assess job opportunities.

"Everyone approaches career planning differently," said Ana Cleveland (professor, School of Library and Information Sciences, University of North Texas). "Some people set goals for their entire career. Some plan out their entire career and know where they want to be in five, ten, and twenty years. They may take extra duties for free to get experience, volunteer, do anything to get that window of opportunity. Others seize opportunities as they come along. Be in the right place at right time; position yourself to learn new skills, and be open to opportunity. Scenario planning can help. Envision where you'd like to be and how you will get there. What skills do you need to be in that position? Who can help you get there? Try to meet with people you admire to ask them strategic planning advice. They may take part in shaping your career by helping you strategize about how you can get where you want to be."

ASSESS YOUR GOALS

J. Michael Farr, in his book *Getting the Job You Really Want: A Step-by-Step Guide*, suggests that you consider what you are willing to accept before considering a job. Ask yourself questions such as:

- Am I willing to relocate? If so, where?
- How much time am I willing to spend at work?
- Are leisure time, family, hobbies, or other interests more or less important than being successful at my job?
- Am I willing to work nights and weekends? Am I willing to work a changing (not fixed) schedule?
- Am I willing to travel for my job?
- How far am I willing to commute to and from work?
- Am I willing to supervise others?
- What is the minimum wage I will accept?
- What job benefits (nonmonetary) are important to me? (For example, tuition reimbursement, health benefits, travel support, etc.)
- Do I enjoy risk or do I prefer a job that offers stability?
- Am I willing to go back to school or earn another degree if necessary?
- What is my ideal job?
- Am I willing to write and publish if necessary?
- What is my ideal working environment?
- Do I prefer to work alone or with groups? In large or small group situations?
- Do I prefer to have direct contact with the public?
- Am I looking for a "stepping stone" or learning experience, or a permanent position?
- Do I want a job that intellectually stimulates me, or do my personal interests fill that need?
- Do I prefer variety or familiarity in my work? Do I enjoy change or prefer routines?

- Do I prefer a structured or unstructured environment?
- Am I comfortable with ambiguity or do I prefer clear directions?

Also, assess your goals. Where do you want to be in ten years? What do you want to accomplish in the next ten years? How could you move closer to this goal in the next two years? Six months? Thirty days?

ASSESS YOUR SKILLS

What skills do you have? Consider your job-related skills, your personal characteristics or personality traits, and your skills that can transfer easily from one type of job to another. Realizing what transferable skills and personality traits you have can help you switch to a new career path, try a new job, or convince your potential employer that you have the necessary skills to learn the job-related skills required for the job you want.

Assessing your skills can be a difficult process. Spend some time alone thinking about specific skills you have learned and what you enjoy. Talk to friends, family, and coworkers to find out what they think you are good at; you may be surprised at what they have noticed.

Think about things you've done in the past (in high school, college, previous jobs, etc.) that give you a great sense of accomplishment. Write a short story or paragraph illustrating the accomplishments you've listed. Review each story and list the specific skills you used to accomplish the thing or skills you developed. Ask others to listen to the story and point out skills. These are the key skills that you are good at and enjoy. Look for jobs that allow you to do these. Mention these skills in your résumé or interview.

Think about jobs you enjoy or jobs that interest you. What jobs do others have that you find interesting? What specific things do you like about that job? What do you like to do in your spare time? What related jobs might use those interests? What previous jobs have you held? What specific things did you like or not like about those jobs? What subjects did you enjoy in school?

Also, assess what skills you can learn or are interested in learning. Read job ads regularly and notice what skills are required for the jobs that interest you. Notice any trends in the job ads; for example, do most academic libraries prefer that you have a second master's degree? Do most jobs mention HTML skills? Talk with people who are in the jobs that interest you. They will often be happy to tell you what skills they feel are important for anyone entering their job. Talk with as many people in the field as possible. Ask what skills they feel are essential and what skills they feel would be helpful. Transferable skills like budgeting, public speaking, bilingual language skills, etc. can put you ahead in any candidate pool. Later chapters cover how you can gain some of these skills early in your career through education, jobs, professional involvement, cross-training, or volunteer opportunities and more.

Tables 1.1, 1.2, and 1.3 list many characteristics and transferable skills. Use these lists to start thinking about your characteristics, skills, likes, and dislikes. What skills do you have?

Table 1.1   Personal Characteristics

- Arrive on time
- Get things done
- Follow instructions from supervisor
- Get along well with coworkers
- Are honest
- Work hard
- Ambition
- Patience
- Assertiveness
- Learn quickly
- Flexibility
- Maturity
- Dependability
- Complete assignments
- Sincerity
- Solve problems
- Friendliness
- Good sense of humor
- Physical strength
- Good sense of direction
- Highly motivated
- Intelligence
- Creativity
- Leadership
- Enthusiasm
- Persistence
- Self-motivation
- Are results-oriented
- Pride in doing a good job
- Willingness to learn new things
- Take responsibility
- Ask questions

Source: Farr, J. Michael. *Getting the Job You Really Want: A Step-by-Step Guide.* Indianapolis, Ind.: JIST Works, Inc. 1995.

Table 1.2   Key Transferable Skills

*Key Skills * *	
Meet deadlines	Speak in public
Supervise others	Accept responsibility
Solve problems	Plan
Understand and control budgets	Instruct others
Manage money	Manage people
Meet the public	Write well
Negotiate	Organize/manage projects

Leadership Skills	
Arrange social functions	Competitive
Decisive	Delegate
Direct others	Explain things to others
Influence others	Initiate new tasks
Make decisions	Manage or direct others
Mediate problems	Motivate people
Negotiate agreements	Planning
Results oriented	Take risks
Run meetings	Self-confident
Self-motivated	Solve problems

Source: Farr, J. Michael. *Getting the Job You Really Want: A Step-by-Step Guide.* Indianapolis, Ind.: JIST Works, Inc. 1995.
* According to Farr, key skills tend to get you higher levels of responsibility or pay.

Table 1.3   Transferable Skills

Skills Dealing with Things	
Assemble things	Am good with hands
Repair things	Use complex equipment

Skills Dealing with Data		
Analyze data	Set up budgets	Evaluate
Calculate/compute	Check for accuracy	Compile
Classify things	Manage money	Investigate
Take inventory	Detail-oriented	Synthesize
Keep financial records	Observe/inspect	

Table 1.3   Transferable Skills (*continued*)

Skills Working with People		
Administer	Care for	Confront others
Counsel people	Demonstrate	Diplomatic
Help others	Have insight	Instruct
Interview people	Kind	Listen
Mentor	Negotiate	Outgoing
Patience	Persuade	Pleasant
Sensitive	Sociable	Supervise
Tactful	Teaching	Tolerant
Tough	Trusting	Understanding

Skills with Words or Ideas	
Articulate	Communicate verbally
Correspond with others	Create new ideas
Design	Edit
Write clearly	Inventive
Library research	Logical
Public speaking	Remember information

Creative/Artistic Skills			
Draw	Paint	Perform	Act
Design	Present creative/artistic ideas		

Source: Farr, J. Michael. *Getting the Job You Really Want: A Step-by-Step Guide.* Indianapolis, Ind.: JIST Works, Inc. 1995.

ASSESS THE JOB MARKET

Now that you're more familiar with your personal skills, look at the job market. What types of skills are required in the jobs that interest you? What types of jobs best utilize the skills that you have? What kinds of jobs are available?

If you are interested in working in a library, ask yourself what type of library interests you—for example, public, academic, corporate, medical, legal, government, association, children's, school, subject-specialized? What type of patron do you enjoy working with—the general public, students, researchers, children, teens, lawyers, etc.? Do you prefer to work with people or with data? What type of role or area of the library interests you—for example, public services, technical services, systems? Do you prefer a small or a large library? What level of responsibility would you prefer? Be aware that some of your preferences will change over time. For example, today you may think you would never want to supervise someone else, but you may find that you enjoy that role after you have mastered your current position.

Are you interested in working outside a traditional library—for example, for a vendor, automation company, bookseller, association, publisher, corporation, LIS program, etc.? In her book *What Else You Can Do with a Library Degree*, Betty-Carol Sellen presents advice from MLS graduates employed in a variety of nontraditional library career options. They include publishers, writers, booksellers, reviewers, vendors, consultants, information brokers, college instructors, grant writers, contract catalogers, information systems designers, association managers, fundraisers, research directors, knowledge engineers, private investigators, archivists, computer technicians, and museum curators. Information professionals have a wider range of options open to them today. "About 40% of recent MLS graduates are taking jobs in nontraditional settings," said American Library Association Executive Director William Gordon in 1999.

MATCHMAKING

After assessing your skills and looking at the jobs that are available, it's time to try to match your skills, interests, and goals with the skills needed for the jobs that are available. The best way to find out what skills are valued for a particular type of job is to read the job ads regularly, even when you are not looking for a new job. Follow the trends. Watch to see what skills are required for various types of jobs. Also, talk with people in the field. Ask if you can visit them at work, or arrange to do some volunteer work to see if you enjoy the area and type of work you are considering.

In her 1997 *Mississippi Libraries* article, Holly Williams asked employers to list the top skills required for entry-level library jobs. For an entry-level technical services job, employers ranked skills in this order: MLS (ALA accredited), knowledge of cataloging tools, prior library experience, experience with automated system, experience with OCLC, microcomputer skills, communication skills, bilingual language abilities, second master's, ability to work with others, experience with serials, Internet skills, and experience with electronic resources. For an entry-level reference or public services job, employers listed skills in this order: MLS (ALA accredited), communication skills, experience with electronic resources, prior library experience, Internet skills, microcomputer skills, second master's, teaching skills, experience with print resources, experience with CD-ROM resources, flexibility, ability to work with others, experience with automated system, bilingual language abilities, experience with on-line databases, and HTML skills.

A DAY IN THE LIFE

Many information professionals in various occupations responded to the questions "What do you do in your job?" and "What would you tell someone wanting to work in your position?" As some respondents wished to keep their names and organizations confidential, the following is a compilation of information provided by people in various types of positions. In some cases, similar types of positions have been condensed into a more generic position category, such as reference librarian.

Reference Librarian

Key Duties: Work with public. Assist at reference desk. Teach library instruction classes. Keep up to date on print and electronic resources. Work flexible hours, nights, and weekends. Sometimes help select materials for the collection.

Key Skills: Patience with public. Ability to explain same thing over and over without condescending. Stamina to stay out at desk long hours. Ability to work nights and weekends. Interest in learning new things. Flexibility to change schedule when needed to cover shortages or emergencies. Comfort with changing technology and resources.

Judy Albert (reference librarian, Ashland University) wrote, "I began work as a reference librarian in July 1999. Some essentials for the job include patience, a sense of humor, attention to detail, the ability to handle many tasks at one time, the ability to listen, a comfort level with asking patrons questions about their research, perseverance in answering difficult questions, and the ability to work both as part of a team and independently. One can always learn the tools of the trade, but these personality/character skills are very important."

Matt Wilcox (epidemiology and public health librarian, Yale University) said, "I have an English MA and I have capitalized on the language and teaching skills I picked up while earning it. It was especially helpful in interviewing because it made the ability to teach a given. Also the study of literature entails reading between the lines to see other meanings than the apparent—something helpful in all areas . . . or at least I like to think so since I went into so much debt to get it."

Stephanie Walker (faculty librarian, Faculty of Dentistry, University of Toronto) cited essential skills for her job as "computer skills, database searching, a decent level of ability to fix minor computer problems, tact, diplomacy, and communication skills. I'd advise people to take all the technical courses they could. Even if they don't work directly in this area, these skills almost ensure employment. I graduated in the worst year ever for employment for librarians at my school, and because of computer skills, I was one of the few to find information management work, if not exactly library work, to start with. I had two years of university computer science programming, which I used in many database creation, design, and management jobs. I have also used the teaching skills I learned when teaching undergraduate English students while earning an MA in English."

Serials Cataloger

Key Duties: Provide access to serial titles in multiple formats in the collection. Maintain the currency of records. Perform authority work. Assist/supervise/train library assistants in record selection and record editing and various projects. Communicate with national agencies as appropriate about various problems (CPSO, PPC liaison, etc.). Solve complex problems.

Key Skills: Attention to detail. Patience to work through often complex problems. Up-to-date knowledge of various relevant cataloging standards and national practices. Broad knowledge of serials cataloging. Diplomacy. Dependability. Ability to meet deadlines and carry through projects. Broad knowledge of e-serials. Ability to coordinate well with various other library functional units (other technical services departments, public services, etc.).

Jean Hirons (CONSER coordinator, Library of Congress) said, "In the past I headed a section of minimal level catalogers and hired a number of people. While I don't hire people anymore, I'm always looking for new talent within the serials community. What I look for are people with energy and vitality, with a positive attitude, an open mind, and willingness to learn and explore new ways of doing things, and people who want to make a contribution to the profession. That contribution may be small or large but the desire to contribute is what is important."

"The most important skills in my job are being organized and being able to deal with people at all levels in a professional but not officious manner," said Wayne Jones (head of serials cataloging, MIT). "Being a cataloging supervisor has, I think, more to do with marshalling the skills of people who work for and with you, than it does with knowing the intricacies and obscurities of cataloging rules and lore. That is not to say that someone who is a cataloging ignoramus could do the job well. I would advise someone who wanted a job like this to work at the working level for a while—do cataloging, get to know the rules intimately, try to understand the context— and also learn how to deal with people."

Systems Librarian

Key Duties: Assist in the implementation, troubleshooting, and support of various networked library systems used for the relation, retrieval, and manipulation of information stored in the library's databases. Inform library staff of system developments and work with appropriate individuals to implement system enhancements and modifications. Provide technical assistance. Prepare documentation, coordinate and conduct systems training. Work closely with programmers and library staff, test and debug software. Draft specifications for programs. Maintain an understanding of the different functional components of the integrated, computer-based library system. Maintain an understanding of national utilities software, library-specific workstation applications, and locally developed products. Assist in the implementation and support of new automated services. Monitor routine databases. Record import, export, and manipulation programs. Maintain system tables. Prepare database analyses and statistical reports.

Key Skills: USMARC record structure. Cataloging rules. NT and UNIX servers. Perl. Basic programming skills (C, C++, Visual Basic, Java, SAS all help). HTML, XML, etc. (EAD, VAR, Dublin Core). OCLC and RLIN Library Management System management. Project management. Supervisory and staff training

Stephanie Schmitt (systems support librarian, Yale University) said, "The pros about my position are that I get to work with all of the departments throughout the library system. I get to interact with all levels of staff and participate in a wide variety of projects. The challenges of the systems environment are the pressure, the instant awareness of success and failures (it works or it doesn't), and the constantly changing environment (office location, personnel turnovers, system upgrades, support application upgrades, etc.)."

Laura Sill (systems librarian, Notre Dame) said, "The skills that are essential for my job are technical skills: thorough understanding of ILS client and configuration tables; 'reading knowledge' of how the programs for the system interact, etc. (although I have two programmer/analysts to ask for help here); UNIX; HTML; communication skills: the ability to explain sometime very complex ideas to general library staff; writing skills; analytical skills; organizational skills; knowledge of library practices (both general trends and local implementation). All of these skill areas come together when trying to support the ILS. They are used daily in problem resolution, priority setting, policy writing, meeting planning, etc. I would advise someone interested in my job to learn as much as possible about UNIX, to concern themselves with what is happening in all areas of the library (not just one or two, although one often finds himself specializing in an area or two), to have some grasp of systems theory (how one part of a system will also impact the whole, etc.). Some skills, like organizational, analytical, writing, communication come with the personality of the individual. I think they are difficult to learn."

Academic Library, Technical Services Manager

Key Duties: Supervise staff. Make vendor selection and place orders. Monitor vendor performance. Deal with especially difficult receipt/order/payment etc. problems. Download bibliographic records for new orders/title changes. Create brief records as needed. Flexibility and ability to work in a continuous learning environment. Work with other department staff regarding questions, problems relating to cataloging, acquisitions, or serials. Set up electronic serials. Communicate with vendors about acquisitions, electronic subscriptions, licenses.

Key Skills: Ability to prioritize. Project management skills. Supervisory skills. Good memory. Excellent oral and written communication. Teaching ability (for training staff). Organization skills.

Susan Davis (head of periodicals, State University of New York at Buffalo) said "My job provides a lot of variety, and I'm surrounded by good folks who make my life easier because they do a good job. I love serials, so I enjoy my work tremendously even when I want to tear out my hair!"

Academic Library, Public Services Manager

Key Duties: Supervise day-to-day activities of a team or department. Supervise staff. Coordinate reference training and desk coverage. Participate in collection development. Participate in library instruction. Serve as liaison to certain academic departments. Participate in library faculty and university governance

Key Skills: Systems thinking. Subject area expertise. Supervisory skills. Strong interpersonal skills. Creativity, flexibility, listening skills, communication skills, diplomacy, patience, teaching skills. Ability to learn, adapt, and teach new technology.

"I work in a team-based environment in a new university. This offers several challenges and benefits," reflected Linda Golian (associate university librarian, Florida Gulf Coast University). "The pros are that team management empowers people, encourages creativity, and allows us to make bad decisions and learn from those decisions. Paraprofessionals are also encouraged to attend training and conferences. I have the ability to work in a new organization that is still creating basic structures. The cons are that true team management takes time to establish and to reach group decisions, and beginning a new organization is filled with many additional hours of work because of start-up issues."

Fran Wilkinson (deputy dean of library services, University of New Mexico) said, "I think that vision, innovation, and being able to think 'out of the box' are all important skills. Being able to communicate and share that vision, leading, and motivating people to get behind it is key. My MPA taught me skills in administration, management, budgeting, and personnel, which are vital. Tact and diplomacy also are important. But I think the skill that has helped me the most is mediation. I was a mediator with Albuquerque Metropolitan Court and I am now CNE with UNM faculty dispute resolution. I am state-certified in mediation and I use those skills everyday in my current job. Also, I once worked as a marketing research supervisor, which helps me with public relations and also conducting surveys. I have done several surveys and published the results."

Public Library Director

Key Duties: Plans, organizes, and directs all personnel. Develops long- and short-range planning strategies. Develops annual budget and presents to county council and then monitors the budget. Plans and performs extensive public relations activities. Supervises the selection and deselection of library materials. Maintains statistical data. Travels a lot as membership in ALA, state association, and Association of Public Library Administrators is required.

Key Skills: Organization and planning. Critical thinking skills. People skills (handling personnel matters is tricky, also needed for PR in the community, also needed for dealing with the county council who holds your purse strings).

Marilyn Tsirigotis (director, Harvin Clarendon County Library) explained, "I am in a small one-building library with six full-time staff and two part-time staff; therefore, I have to pitch in everywhere. For example, I am at the circulation/reference desk eight hours per week, I do my own adult program planning and publicity, I type my own correspondence and put stamps on it, I call tech support for the automated system, etc.

"Some of the pros include being able to lead the direction of the library—for example, I am leading our library to be out in the whole county, not just the county seat where the building is, and am leading it to be more technologically advanced. Meeting and dealing with the state representatives for your district is quite interesting. However, sometimes it is lonely at the top as you have to make the difficult decisions and stick with them. I do not have as much daily contact with our patrons, and because I let my staff work on their own (with some direction), I do not know all the details of how some things are running."

Special Librarian

Key Duties: Provide research and reference services to clientele and staff (this could include corporate employees, physicians, lawyers, etc.). Provide library instruction to users. Manage interlibrary loan services. Manage budget. Manage collection (selection, acquisition, cataloging, shelving, circulation, weeding). Promote library services to users in organization.

Key Skills: Law librarian position often requires legal training or Juris Doctorate in addition to MLS. Other special libraries (for example, medical or corporate) may require experience or background in a certain area (for example, science, medicine, business). Excellent research skills. Extensive experience using subject-specific databases and the Internet. Excellent oral and written communication skills. Teaching and public speaking experience. Strong computer skills. In small special libraries, strong initiative and self-management skills are essential. Organization skills. Communication skills. Public relations skills.

Cindy Scroggins (director, Baylor Health Sciences Library) said, "I cannot overstate the importance of a solid understanding of fiscal management for anyone who plans to direct a library. In fact, I would recommend a fiscal management course for all librarians: the better your understanding of budget processes, the better your ability to take advantage of budget opportunities."

Jennifer Doyle (librarian/Webmaster, Institute for Business and Home Safety) explained, "I chose my current job because of the variety of challenges. In addition to the challenges of being a solo (not totally since my boss, the Asst. VP for Information Services, is the librarian who built the collection; however, I am the one who does most of the acquisitions, cataloging, serials, and a large portion of reference as she has now moved into a higher position), I will have the opportunity to work on the Web site, do some original research, and work on agency projects. I think that essential skills include curiosity and a desire to learn new things. Also, the ability to navigate the huge amount of information resources out there: print, electronic, human, and whatever else might be in store. It is also important to be able to focus on what someone is requesting, which I always thought sounded easy but of course is one of the hardest parts. My advice is to learn and explore as many resources as possible—not necessarily to learn those systems inside and out but to become aware of the variety of capabilities and to be able to compare various systems and resources. The skills that I transferred from my life before library school were the ability to work well with people, an eye for detail, and being able to prioritize and deal with things on a triage basis."

"I think one must always keep up with technology and what is happening in the business world," added Melissa Kash-Holley (librarian, Tulsa Regional Medical Center, L.C. Baxter Library). "One must not only be computer literate but proficient with computers. Learn everything about the Internet that is library related, such as cataloging the Internet (CORC), searching the Internet, the different characteristics of the different search engines, how search engines work, database searching, database design. Learn about computer networks; Marc format; Dublin core; Web site development, design, and maintenance; digital libraries; cataloging in general. Learn the theory and history of librarianship, administration/management skills, interpersonal skills, public relations, grant writing, public speaking. Learn the scientific method of how to do research, gathering statistics, analyzing data, presenting data. Learn collection development (print, media, and Web). Learn Microsoft applications, teaching skills, scientific method for doing research, specialized terminology."

School Librarian

Linda Rowan (librarian, Grey Nun Academy) said, "I work in a pre–K-to-8 private school. I have one part-time clerical assistant, and about twenty volunteers who assist with the younger classes (on a rotating basis). I think I have the ideal job. I have a modified flexible schedule. I teach the younger students pre-K to grade five on a regular schedule each week. My background before becoming a librarian was as a nursery school teacher. I enjoy the story times with my younger classes. The third to fifth-grade students are graded for library class. I teach them information literacy skills in collaboration with their classroom teachers. Some teachers are easier to collaborate with than others. The upper-division students (grades six to eight) are graded for library for one quarter. The sixth-grade students learn the Internet through an on-line activity—the Landmark Game. The seventh-grade students are guided through the steps of writing a research paper. The eighth-grade students write a research paper on a topic of their choice.

"I also enjoy working with the faculty and staff to help them gain technology skills, and to encourage the use of technology in their classrooms. I keep an eye out for good Web sites that I know fit into a teacher's curriculum and then bookmark the sites and make them aware of them. I also pull books and send them to their classrooms upon request to supplement their resources.

"Sometimes in a school library, the only part of the day that is typical is the scheduled part. Everything else hinges on what is happening in the classrooms and the information needs that arise. For example, our five Challenge classes are participating in Australia Quest sponsored by Classroom Connect. That means that every day small groups are coming in to download the latest quest information on the Internet. As they get the information, they need resources to answer questions—and then they're off on a search. When all the free time is used by groups doing research, the library is really the hub of the school. Unfortunately, there are still those jobs to do like checking in and shelving books, working on acquisition and weeding. Sometimes there are not enough hours in the day.

"What does someone need to know before they decide to be a school librarian?" mused Rowan. Her theories are:

1. Flexibility is needed. Things can happen that force changes.
2. Flexible scheduling is the ideal, not necessarily the reality. No librarian should be scheduled to teach six classes a day, but this does happen.

3. A thick skin is good to have. You will hear complaints from teachers who don't like to use technology or don't like the technology that is available. The students will also complain about the materials and technology. Listen to their complaints, and try to add things to the collection that are worthwhile.

4. Definitely visit and try to spend time volunteering in school libraries, if you think that is where you want to be. There are big differences in the grade levels, so you should try to experience all of them, unless you find a good fit in you first experience. It may also pay to find out the differences between a large school district and a small one or an independent school. I don't have to deal with a large bureaucracy and like it that way. Of course, I make less than my public school counterparts, but money isn't everything.

5. Find out what you can about the administration's expectations. Do they want to know every little thing you do or can you be your own boss?

6. Find out what other duties you may be expected to handle. You are just like a teacher and will probably do a recess or lunch duty.

Sales

Key Duties: Establish, develop, and maintain new business with library accounts, including planning on-site visits. Attending conferences. Maintaining ongoing communication and follow-up with established customers and prospects. Develop client relationships and expand network/distributor sales relationships. Coordinate sales effort. Develop and implement sales territory coverage plans. Present company products at all appropriate sales calls. Coordinate follow-up and closing on prioritized open renewal orders and develop prioritized new clients and prospect list. Demonstrate expertise with company products and technologies. Serve as a representative on internal project teams and as a company liaison where appropriate. Provide market feedback for strategic planning and new business development. Conduct weekly reviews of sales plans, weekly sales pipeline updates, and monthly district sales and call reports.

Key Skills: Self-direction, self-motivation, verbal and written communication, diplomacy, persistence. Detailed work, confidentiality, problem solving, constant interruptions, external contacts, persuasion, presentations. Public speaking, exposure to computer screens, keyboard skills. Ability to work alone and manage one's own time. Ability to travel extensively.

"There's a lot of travel—and it's not glamorous!" explained Sharon Cline McKay (representative, SilverPlatter Information, Inc.). "Many weekends are spent either traveling, working, or preparing to do both. Fortunately, my company gives comp time for working weekend days or required travel on a weekend. Whenever I can set my own schedule, I prefer to fly to a major city on Monday morning, visit clients in and near that city for a few days, then fly home either Wednesday (if I'm lucky) or Thursday evening. Then I spend the rest of the week catching up with reports and phone calls that I haven't managed to finish while traveling, planning future trips, filling out my expense reports, doing laundry and going to the cleaners, etc. It's a rare week when I don't have work left over to do during the evenings and/or weekends. When I'm in my home office, I experience a certain amount of isolation because my colleagues within the company are thousands of miles away. We have to work at keeping in touch with each other. As for the traveling, I've been doing this long enough that I know most of the areas I visit and have chosen a favorite hotel and a few good restaurants. I still arm myself with city and state maps (thank heavens for AAA!) and campus maps along with parking regulations, etc., and I still occasionally get lost!

"The benefits of a sales job are getting to visit lots of libraries of various types, meeting and building relationships (and even friendships) with many librarians, learning different ways of doing things, seeing scenery of many different locales, and learning a bit about the various ways of life. Also, the compensation from vendors tends to be better than libraries. The drawbacks include not being able to participate in regular recreational, educational, and entertainment activities such as book clubs, tennis and hiking groups, neighborhood get-togethers due to a great reduction in personal time; experiencing the stress and odd hours of traveling; sleeping in different beds with environments that are sometimes challenging (noisy highways, air conditioners, party animals, etc.); getting lost; and being frustrated that I rarely have time to do anything 'touristy' while I'm in areas with interesting attractions."

Bob Schatz (manager of North American Sales, Everetts) said, "My work has fallen under two broad umbrellas: sales and management. Each one requires its own particular set of skills. Whatever one does, I think it is important that you enjoy your work, that at least some of the basic job requirements come naturally to you, and that you get some satisfaction in your work beyond just earning a paycheck.

"I've seen all sorts of personality types succeed (and fail) in sales. To be good in it, I think you need to have a real liking for people and a desire to be of service. Added to that, you need to have (or develop) good communications skills, especially in writing, which is an area lacking with most salespeople. A good enough intellect to understand the details of what you are selling and the environment into which your product or service will fit is essential. Finally, you have to develop a very disciplined sense of follow-up. Few sales are landed during a single contact. This has to be balanced with a good sense of timing; too much or too little follow up can kill a sale.

"Management has its own requirements," continued Schatz. "Respect for the employees you manage, a willingness to invest the time to listen and communicate with those employees, a sense of fairness, a willingness to represent employee and customer needs and opinions to higher-ups in the organization, an ability to manage stress, and enough flexibility to handle constantly changing priorities."

Project Manager, Automation System Vendor

Key Duties: Provide implementation project management support to customers. Assist assigned accounts in the timely and accurate migration to the company's products.

Key Skills: Strong customer service, conflict resolution, problem solving, priority management skills. Ability to work to immovable deadlines. MLS degree or equivalent work experience. Experience with library automation systems. Knowledge of MARC and its role in an automated system.

Faculty Member

Key Duties: Teach graduate courses in library or information science program. Do research and publish in your area of expertise. Advise students on academic or career issues.

Key Skills: Tolerance for ambiguity, leadership, initiative, self-motivation, understanding of the organization of information or metadata. Public speaking and teaching experience. Self-motivation. Communication skills.

"I encourage students to consider earning a Ph.D. and teaching library science as a career option," urged Philip Turner (dean, School of Library and Information Sciences, University of North Texas). "There is a lot of latitude in what you do if you're entrepreneurial. You can be a free agent, a course designer. Teaching is not a comfortable cushy academic position—it pushes you."

HOW DID I GET HERE?

A few information professionals reflected on their first job and their career paths.

Jean Hirons wrote, "I have been very fortunate in my career in that I basically fell into jobs along the way. From my first job as a cataloger at Southeastern Massachusetts University (now University of Massachusetts Dartmouth) to my present career as CONSER coordinator at the Library of Congress, I've made a giant leap in the relative responsibility of my job, my own sense of my abilities, and my impact on the library community. I attribute this in great part to recognizing what I was good at and making the most of each position as it came along.

"My first realization was that I wasn't like most other catalogers I met. I am more of an extrovert and I like being creative and have a hard time carefully following rules (I write this as I am in the process of rewriting the rules—AACR2!). But I decided that cataloging was a field that I liked well enough and one to which I could make a contribution. As I got to know myself better and understand my strengths, I realized that I needed to find ways of being creative within the cataloging environment. I am fortunate in that both my jobs at the Government Printing Office and the Library of Congress, particularly the latter, have afforded such opportunities. I've learned that writing is a creative endeavor, particularly the creation of the CONSER Cataloging Manual. And that rewriting a set of cataloging rules can also be a very creative challenge.

"I've also learned how much I love to communicate verbally, in the form of teaching, speeches, and just brainstorming with colleagues on the phone. I actually love standing up in front of large audiences! Thus, I've found my niche in the cataloging community. I can do the things that come naturally to me and that not very many 'typical' catalogers would feel comfortable doing.

"So the key point here," continued Hirons, "is understanding what you love to do, what you are good at, and making the most of opportunities that present themselves in your current position. I also must say that having good interpersonal skills has been essential in both getting my jobs and in being successful."

Laura Sill explained why she chose her job. "I have held four different positions during my tenure at Notre Dame, and my reasons for choosing each has been different. Just out of library school, where I concentrated on cataloging, I took a job as Assistant Head of Acquisitions because the job ad called for 'an interest in learning about acquisitions work.' Well, I had an interest. Acquisitions was not covered heavily in library school, so I thought it would be interesting. The position also paid more than any cataloging jobs I was qualified for, probably because of the supervisory responsibilities. I moved from this job to being NOTIS product manager in our Systems Office, after implementing NOTIS Acquisitions as Asst. Head of Acquisitions. I simply found my job evolving, and I found myself spending more and more time on NOTIS-related work (library-wide), and less and less on acquisitions work. I felt I had learned all I was going to be allowed to learn (my boss in Acquisitions wouldn't give me responsibilities for budget, vendor relations, or serials), so I decided it was time to move on. A similar thing happened when I moved from Systems to Head of Serials. My systems job included several cost-benefit analysis projects on our serials operation, and I was interested in a bigger challenge, more administrative responsibility, and the chance to work with serials (which I had wanted to do in my acquisitions days). I chose my current position, after being on maternity leave, realizing that I couldn't adequately run the Serials Department (very demanding), wanted to work only part-time, etc. I am currently a half-time systems librarian for our new library system, Aleph. In this last case, my director gave me a choice of this job and a couple others. I chose it because I thought it suited my background, time availability, etc."

Matt Wilcox shared, "For my first job out of lib school (I am now in my second), I joke that it was just to find out what the letterhead from an Ivy school looked like when they turned you down, but it isn't too far from the truth. I was in the first stages of job hunting and was at the place where you apply only for things that sounds interesting, rather than at the desperate stage of job hunting after many months where you apply for anything that moves. This is one thing I would stress to someone, if the job looks interesting and you think you match it, go for it. The worst that can happen is they chuckle at your résumé and send you a "so sorry, but" letter. Sometimes, places that some people associate with being elite get fewer applications than other places because people sell themselves short and don't apply."

"I didn't choose my job," said Fran Wilkinson, "it chose me. I was working as a paraprofessional at the UNM Library and working on my MPA. I loved the work and kept taking on more responsibility and kept getting promoted. I realized that what I wanted in a job was to lead and manage and to do budgeting and deal with personnel matters. I could do all that as an academic librarian, but there was no library school in New Mexico. Happily for me, University of Arizona started a pilot distance program here in

New Mexico. I applied and received my MLS in one calendar year while working full-time. Around that time the department head for serials at UNM took on the newspaper project and I was offered the acting head of serials position. Several years later the position came open, there was a national search, I applied and was offered the position. Later, Serials merged with Acquisitions and I became director of acquisitions and serials. Then when the associate dean left temporarily, I became the acting and later (when he retired and accepted a director position in Alaska) interim associate dean. I have worked hard and positioned myself at UNM, but timing is everything sometimes."

Linda Rowan said, "I earned an AA in liberal arts, taught nursery school for seven years, then earned a BA in Early Childhood Education and a certification in Elementary Education. For five years, I was a per diem and long-term substitute. I applied for and interviewed for many permanent teaching positions. I noticed a need for school librarians as I perused the want ads weekly. So I entered Drexel University to become a certified school librarian. I hadn't even finished the degree when I was offered my current position as a school librarian. I think my experience as a teacher is a real benefit. I have walked in the teachers' shoes and understand their needs. There is still a need for certified school librarians and I would highly recommend this career path for teachers."

Marilyn Grush (senior assistant librarian, University of Delaware) explained, "I chose my current position when I was looking for relief from my nonsupportive supervisor who was making my life miserable in my previous position. I wished to remain actively involved in interlibrary loan as a professional librarian, something that became very difficult as many heads of ILL positions were given to nonprofessionals. So, in order to remain in a profession position with a connection to ILL, one would need to move up the administrative ladder to supervise all of access services, including ILL, circulation, reserves, stack maintenance—something I did not wish to do. It was when I was teaching Montessori preschool, after my own kids were in college, that I decided to find another interest. As I explored the possibility of a library science path, having previously been employed in libraries during my school career and afterwards, I decided that I needed to actually experience work in a library setting full time again before making a decision to change careers. It so happened that the local university had an opening in the interlibrary loan department. In that position I had a very supportive and knowledgeable supervisor for four years while I combined working in ILL with library science classes that were available locally. Exhausting the local library science classes and being fifteen hours short of the MLS degree, and not being able to leave my job at the regional campus to spend a semester on the main campus, I chose classes to 'fill in' the fifteen hours. Had I been free to spend the semester on the main campus, my focus would have changed to a double degree master's program. However, back in my little narrow box, I finished my MLS degree and began my search for a professional position. Since ILL was the basis of my experience for four years, I searched for an ILL-related position which took me to Chicago, Birmingham, Alabama, Baltimore, and now Newark, Delaware, looking for another supportive and knowledgeable supervisor."

"I quite literally backed into a career in librarianship," laughed Mark Bay (instruction/reference librarian, IUPUI). "I was doing my laundry one day and backed up, bumping a wall. There on the wall was a poster for the SLIS program at Indiana University Bloomington, with little tear-off mail-in cards. I mailed it in, liked what I saw, and the rest is history. As an undergraduate, I wasn't quite sure what I wanted to do with my life, so I took classes in lots of areas, ranging from education to animal science. I wound up with a major in Education, but didn't want to teach in a school setting. I tried nonformal youth organizations, but that wasn't it. In librarianship, I found a career that lets me use my teaching background and where knowing lots of different fields is useful. As for my current position, I wound up where I am because my wife, a doctor of French literature, got a full-time position here in Indiana. The year previously, I was in Texas while she finished her degree in Indiana, and we decided we really needed to be together. So, I applied, and here I am!

"Incidentally," Bay encouraged, "these days librarians have a pretty easy time finding positions where they want to be. Just be patient; you'll get the right one."

SUMMARY

- Assess your goals. Where do you want to be in five to ten years? What is important to you?
- Assess your skills. What talents do you have? What do you enjoy doing?
- Assess the job market. What types of jobs are available? What jobs interest you?
- Assess the skills needed for jobs that interest you. How do your skills match with available jobs?

Table 1.4   On-line Career Planning Resources

Monster.com
    http://www.monster.com/

Job Hunter's Bible (What Color Is Your
Parachute)
    http://www.jobhuntersbible.com/

Occupational Outlook Handbook
    http://stats.bls.gov/ocohome.htm

Occupational Outlook Handbook: Librarians
    http://www.bls.gov/oco/ocos068.htm

Library Science As a Career (Library HQ)

http://www.LibraryHQ.com/libcareer.html

RELATED READINGS

Library Careers

Beile, Penny M. "Other Duties as Assigned: Emerging Trends in the Academic Library Job Market." *College & Research Libraries* 61, no. 4 (July 2000): 336–47.

"Bibliography . . . Jobs and Career Information." *The Unabashed Librarian* 86 (1993): 9–10.

"Career Planning. A Selective Bibliography." *Argus* 16 (June 1987): 59–66.

Casey, Vicki. "Do You Have a Plan?" *Feliciter* 46, no. 4 (2000): 167.

Cates, Jo A. "Managing a Knowledge Management Career Search." *Business and Finance Division Bulletin,* no. 113 (winter 2000): 17–21.

"The Changing Career Scene for Librarians (Web Sites)." *Information Outlook* 2, no. 3 (March 1998): 14.

Crosby, Olivia. "Librarians: Information Experts in the Information Age." *Occupational Outlook Quarterly* 44, no. 4 (winter 2000–01): 1–15.

De La Pena, Kathleen. *Opportunities in Library and Information Science Careers.* Lincolnwood, Ill.: VGM Career Horizons, 1991.

DiMarco, Scott R. "I Know That's What It Said, but It's Not What We Want: The Difficulty of Really Describing a Job." *College & Research Libraries News* 61, no. 6 (June 2000): 503–5.

Eberts, Marjorie, and Margaret Gisler. *Careers for Bookworms and Other Literary Types.* Lincolnwood, Ill.: VGM Career Horizons, 1995.

Goldberg, Tyler Miller. "Application Practices of Recent Academic Library Appointees." *College & Research Libraries* 60, no. 1 (January 1999): 71–7.

Gordon, Rachel Singer, and Sarah L. Nesbeitt. "Who We Are, Where We're Going: A Report from the Front (Career Survey)." *Library Journal* 124, no. 9 (15 May 1999): 36–9.

Horton, Forest Woody. "Extending the Librarian's Domain: A Survey of Emerging Occupational Opportunities for Librarians and Information Professionals," SLA Occasional Paper, 1994.

Kong, Leslie M. "Charting a Career Path in the Information Professions." *College & Research Libraries* 49 (May 1988): 207–16.

Leach, John. "The Career Planning Process." In *Developing Leadership Skills*, edited by Rosie L. Albritton. Englewood, Colo.: Libraries Unlimited, 1990.

Lorenzen, Elizabeth A., ed. *Career Planning and Job Searching in the Information Age*. New York: Haworth Press, 1996.

McDermott, Elizabeth. "A Niceness of Librarians: Attitudinal Barriers to Career Progression (for Women Librarians in Great Britain)." *Library Management* 19, no. 8 (1998): 453–8.

———. "Barriers to Women's Career Progression in LIS (Survey of Working Behavior)." *Library Management* 19, no. 7 (1998): 416–20.

Nesbeitt, Sarah L. "Trends in Internet-Based Library Recruitment: An Introductory Survey." *Internet Reference Services Quarterly* 4, no. 2 (1999): 23–40.

Nesbeitt, Sarah L., and Rachel Singer Gordon. *The Information Professional's Guide to Career Development Online*. Medford, N.J.: Information Today, 2001.

Pantry, Sheila, and Peter Griffiths. *Your Successful LIS Career: Planning Your Career, CVs, Interviews, and Self-Promotion.* London: Library Association Publishing, 1999.

Sellen, Betty-Carol. *What Else You Can Do with a Library Degree: Career Options for the 90s and Beyond*. New York: Neal-Schuman Publishers, 1997.

Wood, Kate. "Genesis of a Career Path for All." *Library Association Record* 94 (September 1992): 592–3.

Specific Careers

Cali, Jeanine R. "Law Firm Librarian Requirements: A Content Analysis of Skills and Qualifications," Thesis, University of North Carolina at Chapel Hill, 2000.

Foreman, Pamela. "Qualifications Needed by Reference Librarians: A Content Analysis and Comparison of Reference Library Job Announcements and Library Science Course Descriptions." Thesis, University of North Carolina at Chapel Hill, 2000.

Holt, Leslie Edmonds. "Dream Jobs: A Career Guide for the Ambitious Children's Librarian." *School Library Journal* 43 (July 1997): 29–31.

Hong, Xu. "What Do Employers Expect? The Educating Systems Librarian Research Project Report 1." *The Electronic Library* 17, no. 3 (June 1999): 171–9.

———. "Whom Do Employers Actually Hire? The Educating Systems Librarian Research Project Report 2." *The Electronic Library* 18, no. 3 (2000): 171–82.

Hosio, Mihoko. "Cataloging Positions in U.S. Academic Libraries: An Analysis of Job Advertisements, 1999." Thesis, University of North Carolina at Chapel Hill, 2000.

Hubbard, Marlis, and Jennifer Tinline. "Career Planning and the Special Librarian: A Selective Bibliography." *Education Libraries* 17 (fall/winter 1993): 14–16.

Lehmann, Vibeke. "Prison Librarians Needed: A Challenging Career for Those with the Right Professional and Human Skills." *IFLA Journal* 26, no. 2 (2000): 123–8.

Leonard, W. Patrick. "On My Mind: An Alternative Career Path to Academic Administration." *The Journal of Academic Librarianship* 13 (May 1987): 102–3.

Moore, Deirdre. "Consultancy: A Career Option for Professional Librarians." *Argus* 24, no. 3 (September/December 1995): 31–5.

Pedley, Paul. "Special Libraries: The Best-Placed Profession to Give Tips on Filtering (Career Prospects for Corporate Librarians)." *Library Association Record* 100, no. 2 (February 1998): 82–3.

Thomas, Alan R. "The Work-Wide Web: A Cataloging Career for Every Librarian?" *Cataloging & Classification Quarterly* 24, no. 1–2 (1997): 5.

"Time for a New Job." *The School Librarian's Workshop* 20, no. 10 (June 2000): 1–2.

Vaughn, Sharon. "One Librarian's Journey into a Cyberspace Career." *The Reference Librarian* 54 (1996): 45–51.

White, Gary W. "Academic Subject Specialist Positions in the United States: A Content Analysis of Announcements from 1990 through 1998." *The Journal of Academic Librarianship* 25, no. 5 (September 1999): 372–82.

——. "Head of Reference Positions in Academic Libraries: A Survey of Job Announcements from 1990 through 1999." *Reference & User Services Quarterly* 39, no. 3 (spring 2000): 265–72.

Williams, Holly. "Required and Preferred Qualifications in Entry-Level Library Position Advertisements." *Mississippi Libraries* 61, no. 4 (winter 1997): 89–91.

General

Boldt, Laurence G. *Zen and the Art of Making a Living: A Practical Guide to Creative Career Design.* New York: Penguin Putnam, 1999.

Bolles, Richard Nelson. *What Color is Your Parachute? A Practical Manual for Job-Hunters and Career Changers.* Berkeley, Calif.: Ten Speed Press, 1998.

Farr, J. Michael. *Getting the Job You Really Want: A Step-by-Step Guide.* Indianapolis, Ind.: JIST Works, 1995.

CHAPTER 2

Job Searching

H.I., you're young and you got your health, what you want with a job?

—Evelle, *Raising Arizona* (1987)

Searching for a job can seem like a full-time job. Job searching is probably one of the most stressful activities we all experience. How do you find jobs that fit your skills and interests? Once you have found those jobs, how do you land an interview and a job offer? How do you assess your potential employer to see if you will enjoy the job? How do you negotiate once you have received a job offer?

FINDING JOBS

Job advertisements are posted in several library journals and many job Web sites. Check not only the library-specific Web sites, but also other general job Web sites. Ask your friends, professors, colleagues, and peers where they found their job. Do you currently work at a library? Find out where your employer advertises. See table 2.1 for some on-line guides to library job sites. Visit these sites regularly—many are updated daily

Tell everyone you know that you are looking for a job. Use your contacts to help you hear about jobs that might not be posted. Don't forget to talk with people in fields other than your own. Vendors can provide wonderful job leads—sometimes they hear of job openings that may not be posted widely. Your family and friends may hear of a great opportunity. Your mentors will usually be glad to keep an eye out for jobs that may interest you, and they will often be glad to put in a good word for you if needed. Get your network working for you.

If you're currently working, how do you let contacts, mentors, and friends know you're job hunting? This varies depending on your situation. If you are in a position that is not jeopardized by your job hunt—let's say that your employers know that you are interested in moving—then you can

Table 2.1   On-line Job Searching Resources

Library-Oriented

Lisjobs.com: Jobs for Library and Information
Professionals
    http://www.lisjobs.com/

Library Job Postings on the Internet
    http://webhost.bridgew.edu/snesbeitt/libraryjobs.htm

Library Job Hunting (Ann's Place)
    http://aerobin.www7.50megs.com/libjob/

Jobs for Information Professionals
    http://web.syr.edu/~jryan/infopro/jobs.html

American Library Association Career Leads
    http://www.ala.org/education/

Chronicle of Higher Education
    http://thisweek.chronicle.com/jobs/

Libjobs: Employment Mailing List for LIS Professionals
    http://www.ifla.org/II/lists/libjobs.htm

Libjobs Career Sites
    http://www.libjobs.com/index2.html

General

Monster.com
    http://monster.com/

Job Hunter's Bible (What Color Is Your Parachute?)
    http://www.jobhuntersbible.com/

be much more open. If you are in a private company or organization, you will have to be much more discreet. Corporate employers may not be willing to keep you if they know you are looking elsewhere.

Bob Schatz said, "People whom you trust, especially those who have switched jobs, will understand your desire to look at other opportunities, and know how delicate that process can be. If you doubt that you can trust someone, don't, unless your current job is not jeopardized by a search for a new one."

Should you keep your job search secret? Should you tell your supervisor you're applying for other jobs, or wait until you have an interview or an offer? Many job search experts recommend that you don't tell your current supervisor that you are looking for another job until you either have an interview or an offer. On the other hand, job search experts also recommend that you tell everyone in your contact circles that you're looking, because you never know who might lead you to a perfect job opportunity. You ultimately have to use your best judgment. It really depends on your situation, your institutional culture, and your relationship with your supervisors. Some places will encourage people to look elsewhere if there is not a good fit for them where they are, or no realistic opportunity for growth. In most cases, your hunt for a new job is your business. At the point where it is most likely to affect you current workplace, it is fair and ethical to let higher-ups know that you are considering or have accepted an offer. A lot depends on how much you want to leave, and whether you feel you owe anything to those for whom you currently work. You have to weigh your own circumstances and relationship with your supervisor and colleagues.

When telling your supervisor or coworkers that you are looking for another job, or that you have one, explain your interest in another job in terms that are not derogatory so that you do not make them defensive. If you have the opportunity to "blame" your move on something external (for example, your spouse wants a job in a different area, or you want to move closer to family, or you want to go back to school and can't do that in your current area), that's often easier for your current employer to accept than the implication that you're just tired of your current job or organization. Some people who have stayed at one place a long time may tend to expect others to do the same. In today's market, however, people are moving around more often and changing jobs more quickly, often about every two years. Moving to a new job can sometimes get you a higher salary more quickly than staying with the same institution.

"[Your supervisors or coworkers] probably don't expect you to stay," said Jennifer Lawley (systems librarian, Cadence Group). "More likely, it's that they want you to stay because you are a great employee. If this is a situation where you feel you need to tell them and they will accept this, then tell your supervisor. If you don't feel comfortable about telling them, there's no reason that you have to tell them before you give your notice. You may be surprised by their reaction. When I changed jobs, I was told that they didn't know why I had stayed as long as I had—they thought I should've moved on to bigger and better things a while ago. They were genuinely very happy for me."

RÉSUMÉ WRITING

For most jobs, you'll be required to submit a résumé. Tailor the résumé and cover letter to each specific job, if possible. Apply for only one position if the library has several openings. Otherwise, you run the risk of appearing directionless. If you do apply for more than one position, apply for each separately, tailoring the cover letter and résumé to each.

Always submit your résumé in the format requested. Pay attention to the format they request and to specific requirements listed in the job ad. For example, some employers ask you to send references or transcripts along with your résumé. Others require you to fill out an application instead of sending a résumé. Some employers, particularly nonlibrary employers, will ask for you to submit your résumé electronically, either by e-mail or by filling out a Web form.

Sarah Nesbeitt (reference/systems librarian, Bridgewater State College) said, "Based on ads that people are sending to me for my library jobs site, 'Library Job Postings on the Internet,' I'd say that more and more libraries are accepting electronic résumés. Many recruiters and placement services that advertise on-line seem to want electronic résumés exclusively (they don't want print résumés at all). I've even seen a number of smaller libraries go this route in order to get responses quickly. A large number of academic and public libraries still want print résumés, though.

"I don't see many employers in the library field scanning in résumés to an internal database," Nesbeitt continued. "That seems to be common practice mostly in corporate libraries where the library's part of a larger company where this is done. Normally employers will specify within a job ad the formats they prefer for e-résumés. If they only provide an e-mail address, applicants should either (1) drop the employer a brief cover letter/query asking what formats are acceptable, or (2) send an e-résumé in ASCII format, within the text of the message, preceded by a brief cover letter. Everyone can receive ASCII, and there can be problems in translation when Word/WordPerfect formats are used."

In his book *Writing Résumés That Work: A How-To Manual for Librarians*, Robert Newlen details the steps you should take to write an outstanding résumé. This book also provides examples of different formats of traditional résumés for various types of library positions. Sarah Nesbeitt and Rachel Singer Gordon cover electronic résumés in detail in their book, *The Information Professional's Guide to Career Development Online*.

Personal Inventory

Use your self-assessment exercises from chapter 1 to create your personal inventory. Not all of this information will appear on your résumé, but think about all your experiences as you make this list.

Professional Work History

List each job you have held, including nonlibrary-related jobs. Include dates that you held each position. List major accomplishments or responsibilities of each position. This is not a job description. Write one-liners to describe what you have accomplished—for example, how many employees have you supervised, how many classes you taught. Did you manage a budget, win awards, get a promotion, hold an interim position, initiate a program, or accomplish something outside required duties? Do you have automation skills, public speaking experience, or writing skills? Quantify accomplishments. "On a résumé, I like to see accomplishments and measured success, and not just a list of job titles," explained Bob Schatz. Account for periods of unemployment. Include consulting or freelance work.

Nonprofessional Work History. This might include student or temporary jobs such as waiting tables. Consider skills learned, particularly transferable skills such as answering telephone or working with people. You may wish to refer back to tables 1.2 and 1.3 for a list of transferable skills.

Education, Specialized Training, Language Skills. List all degrees, schools, and dates of enrollment. List awards, scholarships, fellowships, internships, honor societies, superior grade point average, and extracurricular activities. List significant training courses, dates of completion, and skills acquired. List automation skills and level of proficiency. Include any language skills and level of proficiency. List any professional association involvement; this can quickly set you apart from competition. List positions held in associations, dates held, and accomplishments in committees. Use this opportunity to mention skills not gained on the job—for example, serving as treasurer, chair, etc. Professional involvement can make instant connection with an interviewer who may have similar involvement. Employers who are involved professionally may understand the responsibilities and effort involved.

If you are interested in getting jobs outside of libraries, recognize that library-related companies will understand the MLS and what it represents. Other companies may not understand what skills you have; they often have a stereotype of librarians. You have to explain and sell what you do. Think about the skills you have developed that are useful. Are you well organized? Do you manage projects well? Do you have strong communication skills? How will you sell yourself?

Publications. List anything you have written—books, articles, book reviews, letters to the editor, newsletters for associations, libraries, or other groups. List all publications, even if your publications are all in areas outside librarianship. These show you can publish. Use a consistent, clear citation style for publications. Keep a copy of your publication in case you are asked for a writing sample.

Presentations. List any presentations made at conferences, workshops, and seminars. Include dates held. List courses taught or tours led. Include dates taught when possible.

Research and Grant Activities. List ongoing research. List grants to support research.

Volunteer Work and Personal Interests. List transferable skills such as public speaking, organizational, fundraising, budgeting, publicity, meeting deadlines, training, recruitment, scheduling, leading teams, planning events, coordinating meetings. Volunteer work can show a healthy balance and community involvement. Don't include a "family status" section. Your professional, not personal, life is the focus of your résumé. Don't include a "hobbies" section. You risk being stereotyped or alienating your reader, whose personal interests may run counter to your own.

Sarah Nesbeitt said, "For an academic library job, we have to go through a fairly rigorous process when reviewing a résumé. We match qualifications from the job description to the candidate's experience as listed on his/her résumé. If the candidate has taken the opportunity to tailor his/her résumé to the job description, he or she will come out looking very well. Most candidates don't do this, and I'm always surprised when they don't. I also look for good presentation, grammar, and spelling."

Job Objective

Define your job objective. In his book, Newlen suggests listing a job objective at the top of the résumé. Others advise leaving out the objective statement and including that information in your cover letter. Whether or not you include a job objective on your résumé, it's good for you to define what you're looking for. This helps you focus your résumé on the specific job desired. Tailor a job objective statement to the specific job ad if possible; if not, state type of position held and type of institution desired, so you can apply to several institutions. Keep the statement clear and brief. How do you define your job objective? Think about what you want to do next, in what type of organization, at what level.

"I have always disliked the career objective statement at the beginning of a résumé," said Linda Golian. "I personally find this statement a turn-off when I am hiring because it can sound so general, artificial, and forced. This type of information is much better covered in the cover letter (which many people forget to include—a cover letter is a must. People applying for a job not using a cover letter lose a great opportunity to sell themselves)."

Ann Snoeyenbos (librarian for West European social science, New York University) agreed. "When my colleagues and I look at résumés to decide who should be prescreened and who should be brought in for an interview, the job objective is often the most damning thing about a candidate's résumé. If they put the job that's advertised as their objective, then we think they have no ambition; if they put dean of libraries or some high-level position, then we think they are a climber who'll leave the current position before we've gotten our money's worth. Sometimes a person applies for one job but we think they'd be great for a different job. It's hard to tell if the person would be interested in the second position if they have put down a specific job objective. Leave it off!"

"Although I am not a person who hires," offered Gerald Clark (reference librarian, San Francisco Law Library), "I feel that adding a section on objectives to one's résumé is fine for jobs higher in the administrative order of things. The job objective would, of course, have to be finely tuned to the position/organization you hoped to fill or join. For down and dirty 'you have to know how to catalog, or weed/develop collections, or do reference work, or do other operational activities' types of positions, the applicant's objectives probably will never match the reality encountered in the job in a month, a year, or five years. Nevertheless, you should have objectives . . . just be flexible about them, and maybe they can surface later in a job when you have enough experience to recognize if some aspect of that job might advance you toward their realization."

Summary of Qualifications

Define the skills and qualities needed to meet your job objective. Study the job ad and your job objective. What skills are most desirable for that position?

Review your personal inventory to see what skills you've listed that match the desired skills. Write one-line statements of your accomplishments. Keep the language tight and statements short. Don't use the first person "I." Use incomplete sentences with action verbs. Avoid terms found in job descriptions like "responsible for" or "duties include." Avoid jargon. Don't use obscure abbreviations and acronyms. Quantify accomplishments; be as specific as possible to help employers visualize achievement. Indicate any teamwork or coauthorship. Don't be modest, but don't exaggerate or lie.

Write the summary or highlights of qualifications. Match your most outstanding accomplishments with the most important skills from the job ad. Be brief and to the point. Again, opinions about listing qualification highlights at the top of the résumé differ. Newlen's book recommends highlighting your four major qualifications that relate to the job ad, while others recommend highlighting those qualifications in your cover letter.

"I like qualification highlights," said Bob Schatz. "The job objective and rationale for considering this person should be stated in the cover letter, which should be individually crafted for each résumé submitted."

Donna Hogan (head of reference, University of Texas at San Antonio) disagreed. "I generally skip that part when I review applications and look for the real evidence—education, experience, and some professional involvement—that the person might fit the job we have advertised. A vita or résumé is hard enough to compile into a reasonable length without the addition of information that could be addressed in a cover letter."

Formatting the Résumé

When considering the layout of your résumé, think of it being read quickly. Try skimming it to see if the most important elements stand out. Some search committees must read many résumés, and while they try to give each full attention, they will be more pleased to read yours if it is organized and attractive. Don't allow your résumé's layout to obscure pertinent information. Tailor it to the position. Your reader is probably using a checklist based on the announced qualifications; every relevant item you exclude will result in a negative mark on the checklist.

The most common formats for a résumé include chronological and functional, or a combination of the two. Each format has its own benefits and drawbacks. A chronological résumé is easy to read and shows job progression but may accentuate gaps in job history and may not work for those changing careers. A functional résumé highlights skills categories and draws attention to your accomplishments. This type is particularly useful if you are a student, are changing careers, have gaps in job history or have been at one place a long time. However, some employers are suspicious of this format. A combination format uses the chronological listing, but within each job, uses headings to show areas of accomplishment at that job, rather than straight bullet list of accomplishments. This type can be good for positions held a long time, or for positions that incorporate a variety of types of work.

Put your name, address, e-mail, and phone first. Use your office e-mail if it's not a problem to receive job search information at work. Use your office phone if it's not a problem to receive job offers or calls at work. Be cautious about using your workplace Internet account because others can access your e-mail. Be aware of ethical concerns about personal use of office computer systems.

List the job objective and summary of qualifications next, if you wish to include them. Then list your work experience, education, professional involvement, and any additional headings (awards/honors, presentations, publications, research and grant activities, volunteer experience).

Don't list everything you listed in your personal inventory. Choose the accomplishments that most directly relate to the qualities required for this position. Include all professional experience pertaining to the announced job requirements. Omit irrelevant experience unless you feel something is particularly impressive, though not directly related to the job qualifications. Address anything in your work history that could trigger a question. Your reader won't simply overlook such things as frequent or very regular moves, unexplained gaps, or long periods of seemingly unrelated employment. Don't list each committee membership or internship separately. Instead, put all under the heading of the particular division or organization. Don't list every workshop or seminar ever attended. Omit those irrelevant to the position for which you are applying.

Don't include salary requirements unless they are specifically requested. As mentioned earlier, do not include personal information such as marital status or hobbies.

A one-page résumé is ideal, states Newlen, but two pages are acceptable. Many experts advise against using more than two pages unless writing a curriculum vita for an academic library position. Academic résumés are typically very exhaustive and will include detailed information.

Use plain white or cream paper. Avoid textured paper. Use a laser printer with good dark, sharp print. Employers may photocopy multiple copies for the search committee. Don't print on front and back; employers may miss the second page. Use an appropriate amount of white space and margins. Use bold for headings, bullets for lists, and a plain, easy-to-read typeface.

Sending the Résumé

When mailing your résumé, use a matching envelope if possible, preferably a 9x12 or larger envelope to avoid folding your résumé.

If you need to send your résumé quickly, use overnight mail rather than faxing the résumé so that the résumé is clear. Consider e-mailing a copy of your résumé with a brief, professional message stating that the print résumé will follow. If your résumé is posted on the Web, you could e-mail the prospective employer to say that you are interested in the position, direct him or her to your on-line résumé, and state that a print version of your application materials is in the mail. Some employers will be happy to print your résumé out from an e-mail attachment or Web site. However, send a print copy as well because sometimes your attached files don't look the way you'd expected. Never e-mail a résumé with no attached message; the prospective employer may resent the fact that you have not followed the stated application procedures and may feel that you are asking them to do work you should have done.

Before mailing, do a final check. Proofread the résumé. Check spelling, grammar, and punctuation. Is it neat? Make sure there are no stains or smudges. Have peers or mentors review it.

REFERENCES

Sometimes you are asked to list references when submitting your résumé. Newlen suggests not listing references unless you are asked to do so. Many ads will ask you to submit references along with your résumé. List the person's name, job title, mailing address, e-mail address, phone number, and fax number; many employers contact references by phone or e-mail. When listing references, explain why persons listed as references are qualified to discuss your skills.

When choosing references, never list a reference without obtaining permission first—you want to know they will say nice things. Send your references a copy of your current résumé, cover letter, and the job ad to which you are applying. This lets them know what you have been doing and refreshes their memories about your performance. You don't want them to be caught off guard if the potential employer calls them for a reference! They may also have advice for you or may know something about the job or organization to which you are applying.

"Recently, someone listed me as a reference and didn't tell me about it," said Nancy Cunningham (associate director for public services, Texas A&M University Corpus Christi). "Although I had served as a reference for this person before, I hadn't spoken to him in more than a year. What's more, I knew him only through a short-term project. I received a call from an organization wishing to discuss this person's performance with me. I had to tell the potential employer, honestly, that I had not seen this person in quite awhile and really didn't know much about his current professional performance. I'm sure they must have wondered why he listed me as a reference."

COVER LETTER

Always include a cover letter with your résumé, unless you are filling out a Web application form that does not allow you to include a letter of interest. When writing, think about the employer—what do they want? Use your qualification highlights to point out how you fit the job requirements. Keep the letter short and keep the language tight. The employer will be evaluating your writing skills. Write short, clearly focused paragraphs and be brief in general. Use the résumé to flesh out your qualifications. Your tone should be upbeat, positive, and enthusiastic. You can reveal your personality in the letter, but keep it professional. Use the same paper and typeface as you used in the résumé.

Place address, phone number, and date at the top. Exercise caution when you don't know the name of the hiring individual; use what's listed in the job ad if possible (for example, "search committee" rather than "sir"). Use the correct forms of address for the person to whom the letter is directed (for example, Dr., Ms., Mr., etc.). If you aren't sure, consult the *Directory of Library and Information Professionals*, the organization's Web site, or call the organization and ask. Always address the letter to the person listed in the job ad, or if no name is given, address it to the Search Committee.

Begin the letter by saying why you are writing and how you heard about the job. If possible, use a hook to grab the attention of the readers. Name any mutual friend who referred you to the position. Parallel your experience to the job ad if possible.

In the next paragraph or two, focus on a few qualifications of your résumé that are most important to the employer. Demonstrate what you know about the position or organization and why you are attracted to the position. Again, tailor the letter to the job ad—how you fit the requirements. Don't ask for further information about the library, the university, or the city. If you want more information, do the work yourself.

Gale Hannigan (director, Texas A&M University Learning Resources Center) commented, "I am always impressed with the number of applicants who don't specifically address the job requirements in their cover letter. Meeting those requirements is the basis of the first cut."

Don't go into detail about your current institution's practices unless they supply specific information about your qualifications for the position. Don't use words with negative connotations; for instance, write "some speaking knowledge of Spanish" instead of "limited speaking knowledge of Spanish." Avoid using inaccurate terminology; for example, "on-line searching of CD-ROM products."

In the closing paragraph, end with a positive statement and indicate what you'd like to happen next. For example, conclude with a statement like "I look forward to hearing from you soon. Please contact me at 333-555-9999 or applicant@jobhunt.org."

Don't use humor or "cute" signatures. Tend toward reserve and respect rather than humor or familiarity in your writing. Don't be too casual, familiar, anecdotal, or aggressive. This shows a lack of respect for the audience and the institution. Don't discuss your spouse, children, or other domestic arrangements unless there is a compelling reason to do so. Including such information weakens the impression of professionalism that you are seeking to convey.

Christine De Zelar-Tiedman (assistant librarian, University of Minnesota) said, "Don't apply for a position as a cataloger with a résumé that says your career objective is to be a reference librarian (or vice versa). Don't try to be funny in your cover letter. While this may make your application stand out and some people might find you charming, it can have a negative effect. In a recent search committee I served on, we were using a check-off form to verify qualifications mentioned in the cover letters. One committee member, when she came across someone trying to be clever, asked 'Is there a category for smart-aleck?'"

"Don't use the cover letter to talk the reader through your résumé," advised Ann Snoeyenbos. "Use it to explain things that aren't clearly demonstrated in your résumé, or things that might look suspicious (for example, a four-year gap between jobs—were you in prison or touring the USA in a Chevrolet?).

"Somebody recently asked about how to make it look like you have expertise in a field in which you don't actually know anything," Snoeyenbos continued. "Hey, we do that all the time! And we sometimes hire people who don't have the experience we'd like them to. But we'll hire them because we see that they are willing and eager to learn, that they have skills in other areas that prepare them to take on the new activities, and that they have coping mechanisms that allow them to make it through periods of ignorance or uncertainty without falling apart. How do we know all that? We're not mind readers; the candidate told us in person or in their cover letter."

See table 2.2 for an example of a well-written cover letter, written by an MLS student applying for an entry-level position in an academic library.

Table 2.2   Sample Cover Letter

Dear Ms. Smith,

This letter is in response to your advertisement in the ALA on-line job listings for the position of reference/information literacy librarian. The description matches my abilities and goals, and I would like to relocate to Texas. I offer several years of experience in a variety of positions in academic libraries, as well as an additional advanced degree, excellent computer skills, experience in Web design, and training in user education. My résumé is enclosed for your review.

I am scheduled to receive an MSLS in May 2001 from the School of Information and Library Science (SILS) at the University of North Carolina at Chapel Hill. I currently work in the SILS Library, where I perform various duties including answering reference questions via e-mail and telephone, as well as one-on-one instruction in the use of on-line resources. Coursework in reference, use of resources in the health and social sciences and humanities, Web site design, and user education supplement this experience.

In addition to reference experience, I have collection development experience from the Boston University School of Theology Library. My duties included selecting and ordering new serials titles and assisting the head librarian with deselection and preservation decisions. My employment in the BU Theology Library provided me with a basic familiarity with the processes of tailoring a library's collection to the current and future needs of its community of users. I also possess a master's degree from Boston University in archaeological studies. Earning this degree has given me a grounding in the literatures from such fields as cultural anthropology, Old and New World archaeology, and some aspects of allied subjects such as art history and world history, which will also be an asset in performing any collection development duties.

I am excited by the prospect of working at a university with a reputation for excellence such as Your University. I believe that my experiences, skills, and training make me a strong candidate for the position of reference/information literacy librarian. I appreciate your time and look forward to speaking with you.

With all best wishes,
Clint Chamberlain

INTERVIEWING

Before the Interview

Research the organization. You've already begun this step by researching the organization before writing your cover letter. The *American Library Directory* or a reference guide to higher education can give you a brief overview of the library or academic institution. For an academic position, request a college catalog and information from the admissions office, or find this information on their Web site or at a local library. Familiarize yourself with their college's focus. Look for librarians listed in the faculty/staff directory. Memorize the names of the librarians you will meet.

Does the organization have a Web site? If so, this is often full of information about the organization's focus, services, and staff. Search your local libraries for books or journal articles that either mention the organization or have been written by their staff members. Read all the articles you can find that were written by librarians at the institution. This will not only familiarize you with their work, it may show you the publication expectations at their library. Some employers will send you an introductory packet including information about the library or institution. If so, study this information carefully. Knowing as much as you can about the people you will meet will not only relax you but also will impress your interviewers with your research ability and interest in their organization. Request tourist or relocation information from the Chamber of Commerce, or visit the city's Web site. Scope out the location beforehand if possible. Use contacts to find out as much as possible about the potential interviewers and institution.

"Do your research," emphasized Alison Hopkins (departmental assistant, Extension Services, Queens Borough Public Library). "It always surprises me when I interview candidates who have not looked at our Web site, or who have never gone to their public library. For a public library job that involves general reference, candidates should study up on basic ready reference materials, and best-selling fiction. Candidates should also at least look at an interviewing book and not tell me about their desire to get married, their personal illnesses, their dislike of their last boss, their interest in our benefit package, or their husband not letting them have a job until the kids were raised. Professionalism is important, as well as some interest in the job."

Read books on interviewing to find common interview questions. Table 2.3 lists a few Web sites with questions commonly asked in library interviews. Think about (and maybe write out) your answers to these questions. Ask colleagues and mentors what questions they've been asked, or would ask a candidate, in job interviews. Review the job ad for clues about what's important in this position or organization. Practice interviewing with a friend. If you have to give a presentation at your interview, practice it thoroughly. Time yourself to be sure that you don't talk too long. Practice with any equipment, handouts, or visual tools so that you're comfortable using them in front of a group.

Think of some questions for the interviewer to show your interest in the job, but don't focus on benefits, vacation, salary, and so on. Do not ask about salary; wait for the employer to offer that information, which they will typically do near the close of the interview.

Table 2.3   On-line Interview Resources

Librarian's Job Search Source
    http://www.lisjobs.com/advice.htm

Frequently Asked Interview Questions reported by students at the University
    of South Carolina CLIS
    http://www.libsci.sc.edu/career/invufaqs.htm

Interview Questions from Indiana University Bloomington Libraries
    http://www.indiana.edu/~libpers/interview.html

101+ Commonly Asked Interview Questions from Ann's Place
    http://www7.50megs.com/aerobin/libjob/interview.html

Common Interview Questions listed by Syracuse's School of Information Studies
    http://www.istweb.syr.edu/current/careers/empquestions.shtml

Get a good night's sleep the night before your interview. You need to be refreshed, alert, and cheerful when meeting your interviewers. You'll often need to have good stamina to endure a day or two of extended interviewing. Eat a healthy breakfast (or meal) before your interview.

Dress professionally in order to be taken more seriously. You're safest in subdued colors, styles, and patterns of clothing. Don't let your clothes distract from your message. Navy blue is still one of the most popular colors for interview outfits. However, don't feel compelled to wear navy. Choose a color that flatters your skin and hair color, but stick with neutrals such as navy, gray, black, and khaki. Men should wear business attire such as a suit and tie or jacket and pants. Women should wear fairly traditional business clothing such as a suit or dress. Some corporate employers may interview in "business casual" attire. If you're uncertain, ask. It's typically safer to be too formal than to appear too casually dressed. Don't buy a "power suit" that doesn't fit your style. Wear clothing that you are comfortable in and that looks good on you. You'll be more confident if you don't have to think about your clothes. Don't wear gaudy jewelry, heavy perfume/cologne, ruffled clothing, or anything that makes you look less professional or might "turn off" some of your interviewers. Women, consider tucking a small wallet or purse inside a briefcase to avoid carrying two bags. Carry necessities such as a pain reliever, a comb, copies of your résumé, and samples of your writing or work.

At the Interview

Arrive early. Shake hands firmly, but not too firmly—always be sincere. Smile. Vary the tone of your voice. Relax. Maintain good posture and be enthusiastic and positive. Be yourself. Don't put on a facade. Be as much "yourself" as you can be. It's important that your interviewers know what they're getting and that you know that you'll work well together.

Focusing on the people you're meeting and talking with can help relieve your nervousness. Treat your interviewers like real people. Concentrate on getting to know them as individuals, instead of a faceless mass of interviewers. Try to connect with them. Focus on getting your message across to them, on how they are responding. Listen. Tune in to what issues or questions are important to your interviewers. Listening carefully is especially important on a telephone interview, where you can't rely on visual clues from the interviewers. Don't ramble; stick to the question.

Answer their questions honestly. Guarding your answers or answering only what you think they want to hear will make you appear dishonest. Phrase your answers in a positive light. If you are asked about an unpleasant previous job or your weakest characteristic, be honest and leave your interviewers with a positive impression of your attitude. For example, you might say that speaking to groups is the area in which you need the most improvement, but that you have improved greatly since high school.

"I interview ten to twenty entry-level candidates a month," explained Alison Hopkins. "I tend to start with 'feeler' questions, to find out why they are applying for a public library job and why they became a librarian. I'm usually looking for some thought behind the answers—not a stock or confused response. I usually feel these are the giveaway questions that candidates should be able to handle well. I ask follow-up questions to make candidates feel more comfortable, or if I feel they are hedging—questions like what classes they liked best, what kind of customer service experience they have. I usually ask if they've looked at our Web site, what they think of their local public library, a few situational questions, and some more general questions.

"Throughout the interview, I am trying to discover the personality and interests of the candidate. I assume that most graduates should have similar skills but will need training. I am looking for someone who can be flexible, who is interested in helping others, who wants to learn, who has taken time to prepare for the interview, who has some idea of what public library reference work might be like, who can communicate with others, who is interested in promotion and has some passion and interest in public libraries. I also check for knowledge and interest in best-selling fiction (at any age level), or in popular culture. If someone is good, it usually becomes apparent very quickly. If someone is not doing that well, the interviews tend to go longer as I want to give them a chance—in case they interview poorly or they are a bit nervous."

Gale Hannigan said, "At one organization, we were taught to use the STAR system for interviewing. It is based on the premise that the past predicts the future. So, you ask someone to provide a Situation or Task they found themselves in (for example, can you give an example when you worked on a team with members from other departments?), what Action they took, and what were the Results. It helps avoid the often leading questions or questions where people can answer with generalizations (for example, how do you feel about working across departments?)."

"We ask about the background they have in relation to the job they are applying for, their familiarity and comfort factor with technology, possible research interests (as librarians at our institution are faculty and need to publish for tenure)," offered Christine De Zelar-Tiedman.

In an interview for a sales position, Bob Schatz asks question such as "Who are you, and how does that work to your advantage in a job like this? (If someone tells me that they want to sell to libraries because they love books, I can almost guarantee that they'll fail at the work). I also like to know what direct experience someone has in selling (or managing) and how it demonstrates a good fit for the kind of work for which they are applying. Lastly, I look for how well they will fit into the organization itself. Most failures, I think, are not because the person cannot do the job, but because they have expectations about how the corporate culture will be that are not realistic."

Let your personality shine through. Try not to let nervousness block any signs of life. Your interviewers will remember someone who shows enthusiasm and warmth. In a telephone interview, make your voice sound as energetic, warm, cheerful, and clear as possible. Your interviewers are listening for signs of enthusiasm and interest in the job.

What do interviewers look for in a candidate during an interview?

"During the interview," said Sarah Nesbeitt, "I look for enthusiasm, knowledge, and the ability to present themselves well." Bob Schatz added, "I look for poise, honesty, and excitement for the work."

Ann Ercelawn (original cataloger, Vanderbilt University) offered, "I like to see someone who is eager to learn and knows how to teach themselves new skills. I think this is essential in a rapidly changing environment. Other good personal skills are the ability to really listen, flexibility, a sense of humor, and the ability to accept responsibility for errors and be able to say 'I don't know but I'll try to find out' rather than trying to bluff their way through a new situation. These attributes are much more important than any specific skills you bring to a job, because that job is going to change!"

"I look to see that the person has something to say about the job they are interviewing for," said Laura Sill. "Vision may be too strong for some positions, but I look to see that the person has been thoughtful in preparing for the interview. This may come in the form of having ideas about the current environment, ideas about the area in the context of the overall profession. I want to see some evidence that the person will be a leader, no matter what the position calls for—that the person will make an impact on our library. I also look to see the level of professional involvement and commitment through professional participation. I am more impressed with someone who is actively involved, than the person who just attends conferences."

Don't eat garlic, onions, or other foods with strong odors before or during the interview. Sometimes your interview may take place during a meal. If you're interviewed over a meal, choose your foods carefully—soups and salads can be difficult to eat gracefully. Try to choose foods that cut easily and don't stick in your teeth or stain clothing. Don't drink alcohol.

Be ready with a closing statement in case you have the opportunity to give one. Some interviewers will conclude with the question, "Is there anything else you'd like to say?" This is your opportunity to wrap up the conversation or day with a summary of your interest in the position, understanding of their expectations, and qualifications for the position.

If they have not offered information about the salary or other benefits, you may ask about these things at this time. You may wish to ask about their timetable for hiring. Be sure to show your interest in the position itself, not the benefits that come with the position.

Real-Life Interviews

Ladd Brown (head of acquisitions, Virginia Polytechnic Institute and State University) summarized a typical academic library interview. "The academic hiring process may be defined as glacial, frenzied, and then back to glacial again. The job ad is placed, the closing date nears, the search committee screens résumés, interview schedules are coordinated, candidates are contacted, and travel arrangements are made. The candidate arrives. Then, there is one or two days of interview hell: the travel-weary candidate, who is expected to be bright and glib, is ushered through a tight itinerary, spending a few minutes here and there with deans, department heads, and potential colleagues. Sandwiched in there somewhere is the ubiquitous presentation. It all ends up with an expensive meal that the candidate never tastes. The search committee, using tag-team tactics, keeps up a steady stream of questions and dinnertime chat designed to 'get to know' the now-starving candidate. Once the interview is thankfully over, the waiting begins. Eventually, the search committee concludes its work, recommendations are considered, offers are negotiated, and a start date is agreed upon. The new librarian arrives.

"My favorite part, as an interviewer and also as an interviewee, is the presentation. Usually, the candidate is assigned a topic and they must stand before the library staff and present their viewpoints, or they are given a scenario and they must make believe they are conducting some sort of bibliographic instruction class. For the audience, it is a time to be forgiving and as attentive as possible. For the candidate, it is a chance to show your public speaking skills, teaching aptitude, and ability to remain calm in the face of enemy fire. To make it more interesting to me, I have worked Elvis into my interview presentations. This makes for twice the work: creating the normal presentation to rehearse before the wife and kids, and then reworking it into the Elvis presentation I would do for the interview. Does using Elvis in your presentation always work? Well, not always. It does, however, give the candidate a chance to feel more in control than panicked, a chance to combat nervousness with a little humor. For me, I have to use Elvis in all my presentations now. I guess you could say that I'm 'caught in a trap I can't walk out of,'" laughed Brown.

Janet Foster (Web librarian, Danbury Public Library) described her experience interviewing for a position in a public library in Connecticut. "First, to apply for a job at the public library, applicants go to the city hall, civil service department. There are strict guidelines as to the hours you can apply, start and end dates for applying, and detailed, lengthy applications to fill out. Once the application is completed, you might wait weeks, even months, to hear if your application is being considered for the job. If so, you will receive another impersonal mailing with the date and time, saying to be there at the exact time and date or call to explain why not. Oh, and be sure to call to say you received this notification—nobody is going to contact you, and if you don't respond your name is removed from the list.

"The day of the interview is stressful," Foster continued. "You go to the City Hall Civil Service Office and are greeted by a civil servant who takes away your briefcase (with the nicely printed résumé) so you won't have an advantage over other applicants. You're wearing your best suit and white blouse and mentally going over everything you learned in library school, as a technical assistant—basically everything you've ever known since the day you entered a library as a patron or employee. When your name is called, you enter a room with a long table and a panel of interviewing librarians—three, to be exact. None are from your library, but are volunteers from the community who represent qualified library professionals from the local community—in my case, the panel was the director of the public school's media system, a university librarian, and a local public librarian from a nearby community. My panel members made me feel comfortable and more than one face looked familiar to me . . . and they were all smiling.

"Each member of the panel has a list of predetermined questions that have been made up by the hiring library. Some are quite specific, but many of the questions were personal, situational, or specific to the library—such as why I wanted to work at that particular library. (I had been on the Friends of the Library and had volunteered, so that helped.) After the ten questions, during which all three panelists are madly scribbling notes, I was given an opportunity to speak. 'Is there anything you want to add?' they asked. I think all applicants should be prepared to answer this.

"After the interview, there is more waiting," continued Foster. "The top six applicants are rated with a numeric score and ranked. You receive this in the mail—again, no contact with the library, and the library does not know at this point how you fared. Then the library gets a list of the six people and schedules in-person interviews. Despite my high ranking and score, I was not offered the job. However, another colleague with whom I had worked and who was working part time in the hiring library got the job. I actually thought she was the better candidate for that particular job and congratulated her. A good aspect of the civil service procedure is that all the remaining five candidates are placed on a list for one year for any Librarian I positions and have to be considered first before initiating another hiring process. This worked to my benefit. When the Web librarian position was created, I was interviewed and hired! During this waiting period, I signed on with a librarian contract firm and got more technical expertise, and I worked for a publishing firm, fact-checking books. My advice would be to remain flexible and try all facets of librarianship—technical, patron services, adult, child, medical, school—all experience helps."

"My experience is much different from that of Janet Foster," contributed Victor Schill (assistant branch librarian/children's librarian, Harris County Public Library), "since I already was working within Harris County Public Library when I interviewed for my current position. I am a midlife career change example who moved from book retail into libraries. When I began my employment with HCPL, I worked as a desk assistant at one of the branches. After I had been there for a while, the children's librarian [CL] and her husband moved out of state. Since I had helped her in the past with some of the children's programming, I agreed to fill in and plan and present the preschool story times until a new children's librarian was hired. No one expected that it would take so long to find a suitable replacement, and I performed the duties of the position for about one year and a half before a new CL was hired. During that time, I was reassigned as temporary children's librarian since I was responsible for planning the Summer Reading Program that year. When the new children's librarian was hired, I returned to a desk assistant status.

"Serving as the temporary children's librarian at that branch was the catalyst to motivate me to apply to library school and brave the GRE a good twenty years after earning my BA. Anyway, I did all that and was accepted into the GSLIS at UT-Austin in fall 1988. At that time the UT GSLIS had some all-day classes held every other Saturday during the semester. This was convenient for me since I worked forty hours a week; I could not afford to quit and move to Austin for a full class schedule. I enrolled for one class per semester and drove to Austin one day a week for class. My first two semesters I had the all-day Saturday classes, and later most classes seemed to fall on Wednesdays. Except for a brief period when I was able to count my class time as work time, I used my day off to drive to Austin and attend class. I took the full six years I could use to finish all the requirements for the MLIS, graduating in fall 1995. I was quite fortunate that within two months after graduating, my current position became available. I interviewed for it and here I am. Now, the interviewing process for me (after all the background information) was pretty smooth and low stress level. That's because people already knew me as a HCPL employee and about my efforts at obtaining the MLIS. Any interview brings some stress, but I did not feel alienated by it at all. The branch librarian and assistant county librarian interviewed me, and, as I say, I had a reasonable comfort level—I guess partially that I knew the ACL [assistant county librarian] and had heard good things about the branch librarian. So, my interview was nothing like that of Janet Foster. I guess the bottom line is that my one interviewing experience for a professional position was not an impersonal one, probably because I moved up within the library system from inside rather than outside."

Rachel Singer Gordon (head, Computer Services Department, Franklin Park Public Library) recalled, "On my first interview for a full-time reference position in a public library, I was ushered into the director's office only to come face-to-face with a (very large!) greyhound. I found out later he was a retired racing greyhound that belongs to one of the board members and occasionally comes to the library for a 'visit,' but at the time his presence was rather startling. So, I sat down with the director and assistant director, who proceeded to ask me the typical questions. ('Why do you want to work in a public library? Why do you think you would make a good reference librarian? Describe a situation in which you had to deal with a disgruntled patron and how you handled it' . . . and so on.) Then they asked me how I would feel about taking on 'nonprofessional' duties when needed. Before I could answer, they went off into their own (almost vaudeville) routine about the time the roof sprung a leak and the two of them were up on the roof bailing the library out. This segued into a description of the time they had to call the cops on an unruly patron . . . and the time that the woman who thought the Venusians were after her accused the assistant director of being an alien. . . . So anyway, I should have known the kind of place I was getting myself into right away! But, five years later, I'm still working there—and they're still proving the value of the line: 'Other duties as assigned.'"

Bob Schatz offered this advice to those wanting to work for a library vendor. "Vendor interviews can vary a lot, depending on the culture of the organizations, the personal style of the interviewers, and how desperately they need to fill the position. While it may be more likely than in an academic setting that at least some of the interviews will be one-on-one, there is no guarantee that some sort of group interview will not also take place. Usually companies will want to know more than just background and skills of an interviewee. Depending on the position, there may also be a focus on the applicant's ability to produce measurable results, as well as to gauge his/her comfort with the whole idea of working in the private sector where success is measured via profits. Be prepared to talk about major (and minor) accomplishments, as well as what skills you've acquired along the way. It is also important for applicants with library backgrounds not to seem too rigid or unimaginative. Business realities rarely fit into systems of hard-and-fast rules, so evidence of flexibility is always important. When librarians do not do well in private-sector work, the reason frequently involves the ever-changing, unpredictable quality that comes with trying to show a profit. When you go for an interview, no matter what the setting, try to relax and be yourself. Prospective employers respond well to getting a sense of the person behind the résumé. Even though your future hangs in the balance," he encouraged, "try to enjoy yourself during the interview if you can."

Interview Your Interviewers

It's as important that you find out whether you will like the job as it is for them to find out if they will like you. Most interviewers encourage you to ask questions. Ask them. Have questions prepared in advance. This shows an active interest in how you'll fit into the organization, instead of a desperate plea for "a job." Ask questions that deal with the job duties, expectations, management, or communication styles of the library. Save questions about salary and benefits until late in the interview or until you are actually offered the job. Most interviewers will tell you this information before you leave the interview. In their article "Proactive Interviewing: Strategies for the Assertive Job Hunt," Debra Biggs and Cheryl Terrass Naslund list hundreds of questions you may wish to ask your interviewer.

Listen carefully. Watch the librarians' or employees' interactions with each other. Watch for signs of tension or dysfunction within the organization. Would you like to work with these people at this library or company? Would you fit in with their expectations? Will the job challenge you? Would you be comfortable in this work environment? Use this meeting to evaluate whether you would like the job, should they offer it to you.

Kris Stacy-Bates (science and technology librarian, Iowa State University Library) described some questions she asked in a successful job interview.

"Ask about programs of the library that serve specific groups of patrons. For example, I was interviewing at a state university that is also a land-grant school. This means that my library tries to provide some services that are available to any resident of the state, and I asked about the specifics of this. In your case, the graduate and doctoral students are the most obvious patrons, and the efforts made to serve them will probably be discussed before it's time for you to ask questions. Asking about another group will help fill out the picture—and show you've done some research.

"Ask about the expectations on how much of your time will be spent on each major area of responsibility. If there is an expectation to do research, ask how research time fits in with this. Ask about the procedures and schedule by which you will be evaluated. Try to let your wording and tone here suggest that you see evaluation as a tool for professional growth. Ask about how your potential coworkers are taking opportunities for continuing education or professional development. Base some questions on the position description and specific programs of the academic institution. Ask about what changes are expected for the library in the near future.

"If your interview schedule involves a series of meetings with different people, ask questions in later meetings based on information given to you earlier. Also, the same question may be appropriate to ask in more than one of these meetings. I also was given the opportunity to ask some follow-up questions about a week after the interview, over the phone. I made sure to have some new questions ready.

"With the questions specific to the position description, this was a long list, and I wouldn't have wanted to remember it off the top of my head," continued Stacy-Bates. "I had the whole series, plus more questions that were answered before I asked them, written in a notebook when I went to the interview. Having the notes to look at was very helpful when I was nervous. I had five to eight questions per meeting ready (a number of these were duplicates between meetings), and had time to ask two or three each."

Matt Wilcox said, "I would ask about conference attendance support. Some schools give laughable amounts for conference attendance even if you are presenting or are doing committee work—and these are the same schools that will require such presentations or committee work for promotion purposes. I wouldn't assume that big name schools would support people adequately—they are some of the worst. If they give poor support, you will need to know this so that you can figure it into what you will accept as a salary since you will have to cover what they won't. I also like to know why the last person left the position or how the position came to be open."

"Not only conference attendance," added Jennifer Lawley, "but also continuing education attendance. One of the best ways to be kept up to date on the latest technologies or to learn something new for very little money is to utilize a local consortium, such as Panhandle Library Association Network (PLAN) or Southeast Florida Library Information Network (SEFLIN). There are many other consortiums out there that are state funded and offer many wonderful programs to help librarians. You should find out how much they rely on or utilize their local consortium for continuing education and other programs (like book lending, etc.)."

After the Interview

If possible, thank your interviewers individually before leaving the interview. Consider writing thank you letters to each person who interviewed you. Don't write a thank you letter unless you really mean it and are comfortable doing so—some interviewers feel that these letters can sound insincere if written from a sense of duty. If possible, thank each person individually, either by writing separate letters or by mentioning each person's name in one letter. Recap any major assets about which you'd like to remind them. Correct any issues that you feel might have been misunderstood. However, keep the letter short. Tell them why (and if) you are still interested in the job. Keep the letter brief and positive. Thank you letters are surprisingly rare and can be incredibly effective.

If you don't get the job, some experts recommend that you call or write employer to say you appreciated the opportunity to interview and you would be interested in being considered if other positions open up. Sometimes the first candidate backs out at the last minute and you might be called. Others recommend that you not contact the library if you are rejected. You don't want to seem desperate or bitter. Whatever you do, be gracious and professional. Leave the employer with a positive impression of you because you may see these people again.

"Don't bother interviewing if you aren't excited by the prospect of landing the job," counseled Bob Schatz. "Don't be afraid; interviewing is awkward, but it can provide a great opportunity to receive, as well as impart, information. It is OK to ask questions. Try to be yourself. If you get hired based on false impressions you leave about who you are, it is likely that you will be unhappy in the work, or fail, or both."

JOB OFFERS

When you are offered a job, ask for a few days to consider the offer, even if you are absolutely sure that you want this job. Take that time to think about the position, the salary they have offered, and any other issues you need to consider. Consult with family, trusted advisors, and friends.

If you need to negotiate a higher salary or have other questions, do it at this time. Many employers will expect candidates to ask for a higher salary than they are first offered. Before the interview, you should have consulted salary calculators, places-rated almanacs, mentors, and colleagues to find out what a reasonable salary would be for the specific position and area. Be honest with the employer if you can't live on the salary they are offering you, or if you wish to negotiate for some other benefits, such as on-campus housing or moving expenses. They will counter with another offer, to which you can respond. Many libraries are often not able to negotiate much outside of the stated salary range, but it never hurts to ask. Corporate employers often have much more latitude in hiring and setting salaries. Set priorities in your own mind, and decide what you are willing to accept. Sometimes you may not get the salary you desire, but you may gain other benefits that outweigh that concern (for example, an area with a lower cost of living, tuition reimbursement, a shorter workweek, good health benefits).

Tread carefully in counteroffer territory. Some companies can later resent your forcing them into making a counteroffer to get you to stay at your current job. There are ethical concerns about consciously using a job search to negotiate a higher salary at your current job. If you need to address pay issues in your current job, do so. If you are in a situation where you think working elsewhere is worth considering, then look for a new job under those circumstances. Sometimes an organization will entice you to stay by dangling more money or a promotion. If they do, it is worth considering, but should not be your initial objective.

If you are offered more than one position, or are hoping for an offer from a second institution, be honest with both organizations about your job search status and your interest in their position. The organization will respect you for being honest, and they will tell you how long they can wait for your answer. Some places will be willing to wait for quite some time, while others may press you to make a more immediate decision. You may weigh their responses to this situation when you make your decision about their offers. There is no hard-and-fast rule. You don't have to accept the first offer that comes along; however, you should not expect an institution to hold a job open for you for more than one or two weeks. Set a deadline (for example, promise the employer "I will let you know by this date") and stick to that deadline.

Treat all potential employers with a great deal of courtesy and respect. The library world is a small one, and you will undoubtedly see these people again.

Janet Foster described her hiring process at the public library. "After the date was set, I went to city hall and signed the papers. I was given a union application, a physical, and a start date. Negotiating for salary or benefits is nonexistent. Every Librarian I gets the same exact salary. Raises or non-raises are given to all equally—no merit or bonuses or anything of the sort.

"But what I would tell applicants is: if this is your dream job, which for me it is, look for the hidden benefits," Foster encouraged. "For instance, most companies and libraries in our area have forty-hour work weeks, but ours is thirty-five. The commute is reasonable; [my commute to] one place I worked was one hour and fifteen minutes, and that took its toll. The library promotes ongoing training and conference attendance; we are all given a list of conferences and training and encouraged to apply. Of course, not all librarians can go to all conferences of their choice. The city has to approve the librarian's time away from the city. All in all, though, these are great fringe benefits. The library also has a generous Friend's group that responds to library needs and has been known to help with conference fees at times.

"Check out the mission statement of the library. Mine has an eloquent phrase about 'nurturing the possibilities of your imagination @ the library.'

I've learned so much about technical, people, and building skills at this job that a job with a higher pay rate in another library would not have afforded me. Also, the staff members and director seem to be pleased when I go to conferences and come back with enthusiastic new ideas.

"'Am I lucky?' asked Foster. "Yes. Do I make some of this happen? I believe so. It is sometimes discouraging to work in a union position and feel that staff members at the same level don't have the same amount of responsibility, or see the new librarian with no experience get paid the same as an experienced librarian. But I also feel like the hidden fringe benefits outweigh the monetary gains."

HOW DO YOU KNOW A JOB IS RIGHT FOR YOU?

Be sure your new place is really what you want, and not just something new. At your interview, see if people seem happy. Ask why the last person left. Ask your mentors and contacts if they know anything about the institution. Try to be objective when deciding if this is the right work environment and position for you. Certainly external circumstances affect your decision—perhaps you need a job and don't care what it is; perhaps you want to relocate for personal reasons. Still, try to decide if the position and workplace fits your personality, interests, and work styles; you will be much more productive and the employer will be much happier with you if you find the right match.

"I continue to be surprised by the number of people who tell me about interviews where they are not introduced to library staff or given a full tour of the library," said Cindy Scroggins. "My advice is *never* to accept a position without having been given the opportunity to speak to the people you will be working with. This is especially important if the position involves supervision of others—if the interviewers do not want you to meet the people you will supervise, run!"

Alison Hopkins said, "It's hard for a candidate to assess their potential workplace at my institution—I hire for sixty-two locations. I tend to look at the large public libraries as fairly similar—a good place to gain experience in public libraries with some possibilities for promotions. For me, I judge the interviewer. I look at what kinds of questions I am asked, the atmosphere of the office (Is it formal? Informal? How does the secretary behave? Is the phone ringing constantly? Is the interviewer organized?), How are people dressed? Are personal objects on people's desks? (Too many? None?). Then I consider what I am looking for—I want to meet my supervisor (at this stage in the game, maybe not as entry-level, depending on the library) and I want to know what kind of person she is looking for. I enjoy change, so I will ask how the library has reacted to changes in the information environment, if conference attendance is supported, how the staff interacts with their public, etc.

"When I choose my current position," Hopkins explained, "I had interviewed with two library systems, Brooklyn and Queens, and received two job offers. I made my decision based on the interviewing styles. Brooklyn's interview consisted of an hour of questions, mostly concerning my ability to survive in New York City, and then an instant offer of employment. Queens gave me a tour of several branches and I was interviewed by a whole series of people. I felt as if Queens took me as a candidate more seriously, and so I accepted their job offer."

Laura Sill mused, "How do you know if a job is right for you? I believe this can only happen if you decide what you want to see happen in the position you are applying for. If you know your vision for yourself in the job, prepare questions that fit that vision, then you will see where you have differences with the actual environment. One word of advice I can give here, and perhaps others would disagree—where you see differences, really think hard about whether these are areas you can change to fit your vision. Some things (attitudes, behaviors, etc.) are very difficult to change. While you may really want the position, if the areas where there are differences are those that can't be changed, you may be better off looking for a better fit to your vision and the environment."

"Trust your instincts," urged Bob Schatz. "If you feel discomfort and have to talk yourself into wanting the work, there is something wrong. If you worry about what it would be like to work for a particular supervisor, there's probably a reason for that. If you feel stress just thinking about how that organization defines success, you'll probably feel even more stress in the work itself. Never want a job so badly that you'll take one that doesn't feel right for you."

QUITTING YOUR JOB

Don't quit a job unless you have a new one, if you can help it. Be cautious about what you say about your current job. Don't resign unless you really mean it. Check your institution's policy for resigning. Some organizations will have rules stating how much notice you have to give before leaving your current job. If your employer does not state this, give at least two weeks' notice before moving on.

Don't be surprised if people are upset with you when you announce you are leaving. You have just said you no longer want to be part of their organization. Some bosses feel personally rejected (whether or not they realize it) when their employees quit. Never burn bridges at your former job; the library field is a small place and you'll need those contacts later. Still, don't be surprised if your former supervisors or colleagues feel some resentment; you're putting a hardship on them by leaving, and some people take your leaving as a personal rejection.

Thank the people who have helped you at the job you are leaving. Stay in touch with former supervisors, mentors, and colleagues, if possible. They will remember you fondly later when you need references or contacts.

AFTER YOU ARE HIRED

Always keep your résumé current. You never know when you will need it for an annual review, a promotion, tenure documentation, an award application, a grant application, and so on. Keeping your résumé current and supporting documentation on hand also prepares you in case that ideal job opportunity drops into your lap.

SUMMARY

- When searching, use your network to help you hear of opportunities.
- Use discretion when telling supervisors or coworkers that you are searching for a job.
- Tailor your résumé and cover letter to each individual job opening.
- Ask your references before providing their names to potential employers.
- Do your research, practice your answers, and prepare your questions before an interview.
- During the interview, interview your interviewers, so that you will both be able to judge how well you will work together.
- When you are offered a job, negotiate for any benefits you feel are essential, and take time to consider the offer before accepting.
- Treat your current employer with courtesy and honesty when submitting your resignation.

RELATED READING

Job Searching

Anderson, James F. "Didn't You Learn That in Library School? (Expectations of Library Directors for Job Applicants)." *Mississippi Libraries* 61, no. 4 (winter 1997): 87–8.

Ballard, Terry. "We're Honored That You Applied Here (Librarians' Employment Searches)" *Information Today* 15, no. 2 (February 1998): 4.

Beile, Penny M. "Other Duties As Assigned: Emerging Trends in the Academic Library Job Market." *College & Research Libraries* 61, no. 4 (July 2000): 336–47.

Cates, Jo A. "Managing a Knowledge Management Career Search." *Business and Finance Division Bulletin* no.113 (winter 2000): 17–21.

DiMarco, Scott R. "I Know That's What It Said, but It's Not What We Want: The Difficulty of Really Describing a Job." *College & Research Libraries News* 61, no. 6 (June 2000): 503–5.

Foster, Janet B. "Jobs on the Net for Librarians." *Public Libraries* 38, no. 1 (January/February 1999): 27–9.

Fox, Charlie. "Employment & Job Search." *Library Mosaics* 10, no. 3 (May/June 1999): 5–19.

Goldberg, Tyler Miller. "Application Practices of Recent Academic Library Appointees." *College & Research Libraries* 60, no. 1 (January 1999): 71–7

Gordon, Rachel Singer, ed. "The Library Job Hunt." *Info Career Trends* 2, no. 1 (January 2001) <http://lisjobs.com/newsletter/archives.htm> (1 Mar 2001). The entire issue deals with job hunting.

Hacken, Richard D. "Finding Your Proper Niche in the Bibliotheca Academiae; or, The Study of Elephant Hunting Behavior." *Collection Management* 17, no. 3 (1993): 25–7.

Howze, Philip C. "10 Job-Hunting Tips for New Librarians." *College & Research Libraries News,* no. 7 (July/August 1997): 490–2.

Johnson, Linda C. "What Personal Traits Do Job Advertisements Seek? And Do They Correlate with Myers-Briggs Type Indicators?" Thesis, University of North Carolina at Chapel Hill, 1994.

Larsen, Suzanne T., and Joan S. McConkey. "Applying for Professional Positions (How to Present Your Assets in the Most Favorable Light)." *College & Research Libraries News,* no. 6 (June 1995): 415–7.

Lorenzen, Elizabeth A. "Librarian for Hire: Internet Surfing for Job Search Success." *Technicalities* 15 (January 1995): 11–4.

MacAdam, Carol. "Job Hunter's Workshop: How to Find and Land the Right Job, and Survive the Transition (Workshop Report from the 1994 NASIG Conference)." *The Serials Librarian* 25, no. 3–4 (1995): 357–61.

Nesbeitt, Sarah L. "Trends in Internet-Based Library Recruitment: An Introductory Survey." *Internet Reference Services Quarterly* 4, no. 2 (1999): 23–40.

"Other Duties As Assigned." *The Unabashed Librarian,* no. 113 (1999): 24–5.

Roberts, Joni R. "Have I Got a Job for You! Common Sense Tips for Getting Your Foot in the Door." *Library Mosaics* 10, no. 3 (May/June 1999): 14–5.

Rosenthal, Marilyn G. "Making Short Work of the Job Search." *Library Journal* 122 (1 September 1997): 145–8.

Saunders, Kay Carolyn. "How to (Survive until You) Get a Library Job (Experience of a New Library School Graduate)." *Public Library Quarterly* 14, no. 4 (1995): 21–6.

Scherrei, Rita A. "Strategies for the Job Search." *Library Mosaics* 4 (March/April 1993): 8–10.

Singer, Rachel. "Neglected Networking: Why (and How!) Not to Overlook the Internet in Your Library Job Search." *Illinois Libraries* 79 (fall 1997): 174–7.

Stroyan, Sue. "Qualifications Sought by Employers of Health Sciences Librarians, 1986." *Bulletin of the Medical Library Association* 75 (July 1987): 209–13.

White, Dan A., and Maureen White. "Getting the Job: What School Library Directors Look for in Applicants. (Junior Members Round Table Panel Discussion at the 1989 Texas Library Association Conference)." *The School Librarian's Workshop* 10 (May 1990): 3–4.

White, Gary W. "Academic Subject Specialist Positions in the United States: A Content Analysis of Announcements from 1990 through 1998." *The Journal of Academic Librarianship* 25, no. 5 (September 1999): 372–82.

———. "Head of Reference Positions in Academic Libraries: A Survey of Job Announcements from 1990 through 1999." *Reference & User Services Quarterly* 39, no. 3 (spring 2000): 265–72.

Williams, Holly. "Required and Preferred Qualifications in Entry-Level Library Position Advertisements (Analysis of Ads in Recent Issues of American Libraries and Library Journal)." *Mississippi Libraries* 61, no. 4 (winter 1997): 89–91.

Wong, Clark C. "Job Search: Strategies to Improve Your Success Rate." *Ohio Media Spectrum* 40 (spring 1988): 40–3.

Worlton, Colleen. "A Plan for Marketing Yourself." *Library Mosaics* 4 (March/April 1993): 17.

Résumé Writing

Brooks, Michael D. "The Résumé: More Than Words on a Page." *Library Mosaics* 10, no. 3 (May/June 1999): 16–17

McKay, Beatrice L. and Clare Dunkle. "Top of the Heap or Bottom of the (Trash) Barrel? Tips for Job Applicants. *NMRT Footnotes* 22, no.2 (January 1993). <http://www.ala.org/nmrt/footnotes/applicants.html> (1 March 2001).

Nesbeitt, Sarah, and Rachel Singer Gordon. *The Information Professional's Guide to Career Development Online.* Medford, N.J.: Information Today, 2001. Includes chapters on electronic résumés and job hunting on-line.

Newlen, Robert R. *Writing Résumés That Work: A How-to-Do-It Manual for Librarians*. New York: Neal-Schuman Publishers, 1998. Includes practical tips and samples of various types of résumés for library jobs.

Ream, Richard. "Rules for Electronic Résumés." *Information Today* 17, no. 8 (September 2000): 24–5.

Womack, Kay, and Tyler Miller Goldberg. "Résumé Content: Applicants' Perceptions." *College & Research Libraries* 58 (November 1997): 540–9.

Interviewing

Biggs, Debra R., and Cheryl Terrass Naslund. "Proactive Interviewing: Strategies for the Assertive Job Hunt." *College & Research Libraries News*, no. 1 (January 1987): 13–17. Includes more than 100 questions a candidate might ask a prospective interviewer.

Collins, Sandra. "They Want to Talk to Me? Surviving Your First Professional Interview." *Library Journal* 120 (15 October 1995): 34–5.

Dinerman, Gloria. "The DISRAELI Method: The Absolutely Foolproof Way to Hire (Method of Hiring Staff Which Looks at Personal Qualities during Interviews)." *Library Management* 16, no. 6 (1995): 33–6.

"EEOC Issues ADA Guidelines on Job Interviews." *Library Personnel News* 9 (January/February 1995): 3–4.

Kimmel, Stacey E., and Scott R. DiMarco. "Planning an Interview: What Do Candidates Want?" *College & Research Libraries News*, no. 4 (April 1997): 249–50.

Klob, Priscilla. "First Impressions, Lasting Impressions: Tips for Job Interviews." *NMRT Footnotes* 26, no.2 (January 1997). <http://www.ala.org/nmrt/footnotes/interview.html> (1 March 2001).

Myers, Margaret. "Job Hunting Strategies for Power Interviews and Résumés." In *Culture Keepers*. Chicago, Ill.: Black Caucus of the American Library Association, 1993.

Russell, Thyra Kaye. "Interviewing (Candidates)." In *Practical Help for New Supervisors,* edited by Joan Giesecke. Chicago, Ill.: American Library Association, 1997.

Tripp, Carol. "Be Prepared and Interview with Confidence." *Library Mosaics* 10, no. 3 (May/June 1999): 8–11.

CHAPTER 3

Experience and Education

Every moment in life is a learning experience. Or what good is it, right?

—Paul, *Six Degrees of Separation* (1993)

In the early stages of your career, it is especially important to learn all you can and to prepare yourself to move in different directions as you find out what you do and do not enjoy. Diversify your experience and education to provide a broad framework for the future. Give yourself room to change your mind or accept a variety of opportunities. Learn to manage your time, projects, and stress as you cope with the inevitable changes in your life, your career, and the library world. As you accumulate experience and education, learn to market your new abilities and knowledge effectively.

EXPERIENCE

Student or Internship Experience

Try to get a job or internship, or volunteer in order to get relevant experience while in school. Talk to coworkers to find out how they like their jobs. Find out about different types of jobs in the field. Getting experience in school will also help make your classes more relevant.

"As a student," said Jennifer Doyle, "I took advantage of the many preprofessional jobs that were available. Over a year and a half, I worked at a historical society, a multinational consulting firm, and an insurance industry association. In addition to being able to hone the skills that I was learning in classes (most notably cataloging), I was exposed to so many different experiences that I felt comfortable making a decision as to which type of institution I'd like to work for. Because of my experience in these jobs, I was able to confidently state my abilities in my job interviews as well as offer quite a bit once I started, even though I was a brand new graduate."

Barb Anderson (systems librarian, Shawnee State University) wrote, "Having come from the world of programming (nice money, unreal stress levels) I have come to value doing something I enjoy over money. My recommendation would be to sample lots of areas via classes and see what you enjoy the most. You may be surprised. This field has put the joy back into computers for me. If you have the opportunity to volunteer, take an internship, do a practicum, etc. while you are in school, do it! They can be invaluable to give you a better feel for an area you are considering. If at all possible, tour lots and lots of different sorts of libraries and ask questions— the touring sponsored by the local ASIS and SLA chapters in conjunction with meetings was very enriching, as were the many tours and visits scheduled by our student organizations while I was in school.

"Being a systems librarian isn't always a guarantee of big bucks," cautioned Anderson. "Some appallingly low offers show up quite often on various lists, and many smaller places pay poorly. Employees can get more experience and often don't stay long at such places. I just can't emphasize enough the importance of doing something you truly like, enjoy, love (hopefully the latter) for a living. It makes such a difference!"

Bob Schatz said, "Few of the skills I've had to develop in my professional work were addressed in library school. My master's degree gave me a working vocabulary in librarianship, and provided me with some useful contacts. There was little there, though, that prepared me for what work in real life was all about. Most of that has come to me through trial and error and, to a lesser degree, from being mentored. The professional library program I received in school gave a false impression that real working environments have stable rules and predictable processes dealing with demands. While work environments do have basic structures within which the work takes place, within that there is a great degree of unpredictability that I was not prepared for. Learning how to put that to work to my advantage took a long time, and did not come easily."

"I held around four student positions while I was in library school," reminisced Sarah Nesbeitt. "I hadn't worked in a library before this time, so all of the experience I got was very helpful (and no doubt looked better on a résumé than if I'd gone job hunting after the MLS without any library experience). I interned at the undergraduate library at the University of Michigan, which involved being at the reference desk there for twenty hours/week. There, I learned the typical questions asked of undergraduates, and I got comfortable being there. I also did volunteer work setting up a library for a local nonprofit agency, and there I learned the typical reference sources used by nonprofits. I've used those skills at my current job, doing workshops for the Grants Office there on how to search the *Federal Register.*"

Workplace or Volunteer Experience

Work or volunteer at different types of libraries or organizations to gain experience and see what type of environment you like. Get a variety of experience, if possible, to provide a diversity of options and a broader perspective. Volunteer for committee work, task forces, or special projects to get varied types of responsibilities and experience. Work with different people to get different perspectives both on their type of job and on working with different styles of people and in different atmospheres. Ask your supervisor if you can cross-train in another department.

Gerald Clark said, "Looking at the long term, I would urge you to start getting the type(s) of experience required/preferred by the positions you want to move in to. Quite likely, you will have to volunteer evenings or weekends to acquire it. However, you will come away with the experience, and you will have demonstrated to potential employers that you have the interest and commitment to the field/subject. As an example, when I graduated in May 1999, I knew I wanted to do reference work in public/academic/special libraries. I had, however, a full-time job in technical services. I searched around for someplace that would accept a postgraduate volunteer. It wasn't easy: most academic libraries in the San Francisco area wouldn't accept someone not currently in library school, or they just simply said they couldn't be bothered. But the University of San Francisco did accept me and I volunteered there two evenings a week for a school year. This was a pain on top of a full-time day job, but when I finished I had made many new friends, had had a great training experience, and knew that this was, indeed, the kind of work I wanted to do. "

Often, small libraries can offer you more variety, because you get to do a little of everything. If you work in a large institution, ask if you can volunteer in a different department in your own library. By trying different things, then you can assess what you like and don't like, and decide what you might like to do next. Don't be surprised if you change types of jobs often during your first ten years or so. These are your learning years and by trying different things, you learn about different types of jobs. Also, by diversifying your experience, you don't get pigeonholed into a niche that you later can't break out of.

Judy Albert commented, "I came to librarianship from the field of education, and to academic librarianship from public education. Many skills of a teacher/school librarian are applicable to my current position. My internship allowed me to learn many skills that have transferred to my current job. I gained knowledge of the most popular and useful academic reference tools, as well as those needed by the general public, because our library is heavily used by community members. Much more importantly, I learned how to interact with patrons; I observed a number of differing public service styles and approaches, and I was able to develop my own philosophy of public service. I made valuable contacts in the field, and many wonderful friendships. A testament to the success of this program, I think, is the fact that all of the students who interned with me during my year of graduate school, approximately a dozen students, are currently working in the field, most in academic libraries, a few in public."

"In library school, I took classes that interested me," Erin Hanley (technical services/systems librarian, Mercyhurst College) said. " Aside from the basics (reference, cataloging, statistics, etc.), I took classes in everything from children's literature to rare books to legal and government research. I'm not sure how that has affected my marketability, but I know that it made my education a lot more enjoyable, and it taught me how to apply skills learned in one area to another. One option, if you're not ready to assign yourself the title of 'cataloger' or 'reference librarian,' is to find a position where you can do and learn a bit of everything."

Richard Murray (catalog librarian, Vanderbilt University Library) advised, "If you decide that technical services is where you want to be, I would recommend getting as much hands-on practical experience as you possibly can while you're in school. If you want to be a cataloger, for example, and you come out of library school having taken as many classes as possible on cataloging, you've got some real life experience in a catalog department, you can toss around terms like OCLC and NACO and PCC and know what you're talking about, and you are genuinely enthusiastic about cataloging, I bet you won't have too hard a time finding a job—especially if you're willing to relocate.

"If you don't know what you want to do, I'd recommend trying your hand at a number of different things through part-time jobs, student assistant positions, volunteering, or whatever. Maybe you'll stumble into something you find out you really enjoy. And if not," Murray mused, "I think that finding out what you don't want to do is just as important as finding out what you do want to do."

Professional Involvement Experience

Use professional or community involvement to gain experience. You can use these activities to gain experience in areas that you are not able to gain at work or school. For example, you may be able to participate on a committee that allows you to learn to manage a budget, plan programs, manage projects, work with teams, write for publications, speak in public, run meetings, create Web pages, and more. Try to get varied experience in your association work. Look for ways to build skills that you aren't able to build in your daily job. Don't forget to list these skills in your résumé.

Serve on search committees to see résumés, interviews, and search processes. Serve on award committees to see applications and selection processes. Serving on search or selection committees allows you to see what your colleagues and supervisors notice in résumés. It allows you to see others' résumés, and allows you to learn for your own future job interviews. Watch what your colleagues or supervisors notice, like, and dislike as they select candidates for job interviews or awards.

Sarah Nesbeitt described how serving on search committees helped her. "I've been on at least six search committees at my library and chaired two. I enjoy doing this, because I like seeing the employment process from the other side, looking at candidates' experiences and how they can best fit the position. At an academic library, I learned to work within the system to be able to hire the candidate chosen by the group. Everything has to be very well documented and we have a whole Affirmative Action process to go through. You have to give explicit reasons (or at least have them in mind, should anyone later ask about it) why a particular candidate was chosen and others weren't."

Public speaking can be one of the most difficult tasks for many people. If you find this daunting, take opportunities to speak in public. Teach classes, speak in meetings, and take opportunities to practice speaking to groups. Professional association involvement may give you the opportunity to host programs or speak at various meetings. Accept these invitations to try to build confidence in front of people.

"I've been on so many committees in my library system," said Alison Hopkins, "and every one has been really important in my career. I suppose the one that helped the most was the Internet Self-Managed Work Team. The committee was an experiment in my library system—there were seven members, all fairly new librarians who worked together to incorporate Internet usage in the library system. As part of that committee, I learned how the administrative structure of the library worked, made presentations to department heads, presented poster sessions at ALA, had articles published, and presented two programs at the state library conference. It was a very positive experience."

ON THE JOB

How well you do on your first job and the lessons you learn there will make a difference in your work habits and career. You will move from one entry-level experience to another if you don't figure out how to handle that first job well, said Eve Luppert in her book, *Rules for the Road: Surviving Your First Job Out of School*. Learn from every manager, good and bad, every assignment, and every situation. You can learn even from the worst job or manager.

Organizational Culture

When starting a new job, figure out the rhythm of the company. Try to get your workday synchronized with others so you don't miss out on important conversations or jobs. For example, if important news tends to be passed around early in the morning, you don't want to miss out on these conversations by arriving late every day. Are you expected to stay late or work weekends? Are there social breaks where interdepartmental news is shared informally? Pay attention to what's sacred, what's accepted, and what's never done.

"In your first job, you usually have very little control over your career or your job choice," said Beverley Geer (metadata librarian, Questia Media Inc.). "During the first few years in your new job, get accustomed to the organizational culture. Take time to find out whether the job suits you. Understand and get to know system and environment. Honor the lines of communication. Keep an eye out for when you are being taken advantage of. Don't be afraid to express your dissent. Watch how people interact. Find out who's effective in getting things done."

Bob Schatz added, "Librarians may not have realistic expectations of what private sector work is like. It's not as organized as we may want the setting to be. There may be no rules because no one has done it before. Some librarians find it hard to embrace the for-profit motive; it's not the same service ethic. Get used to being flexible in whatever arena you work. There are ethical battles over resources, structural issues, service issues.

Sometimes librarians feel they have to compromise service ethics they learned in library school when they are working in the business world.

"In academe," continued Schatz, "it is sometimes hard to define success. The library doesn't bring in grants and money, as a for-profit business would. Don't lose the sense of the bigger environment, of how the library fits into the entire institution. Be careful not to threaten the status of others in the larger context, or walk into something you weren't expecting. Expect slow progress in academe. Take baby steps, establish yourself, build a reputation, build a relationship with others, establish yourself and your agenda, and start moving."

Find out your organizational culture regarding socializing at work and with your coworkers. Typically, socializing is fine, as long as it doesn't distract you or others from their work. However, be careful about becoming too friendly with those you supervise; keep those relationships on a professional level while at work. Sometimes, developing a close friendship with people who report to you can cause problems. Other employees may perceive that you are playing favorites. It may be harder for you to discipline an employee who is not performing at the level they should, if you are friends with that employee. They may take advantage of your friendship by slacking off, not taking your instructions seriously, or taking your criticisms too personally.

However, this doesn't mean you can't socialize and become friends with colleagues—often you will form lasting friendships with coworkers. You spend most of your day with your coworkers, and in the best situations, you will become close to these people. In an ideal working environment, you will enjoy going to work to be around your colleagues. Treating your fellow employees as peers or even as friends can engender trust and loyalty. When you have responsible people working with you, you can be much more relaxed and friendly with them, because you know that they are going to do their job. However, be careful about jumping into friendships, at least with those you supervise, until you have watched their performance and established yourself as an impartial supervisor. When dealing with your peers and supervisors, take time to get to know how everyone interacts. Ally yourself with people whom you enjoy, but beware of forming cliques. Try to treat everyone the same. Don't expect special favors if you work for a friend.

Environments and organizational cultures change, sometimes very rapidly. The job you sign up for may be very different two months later. Your boss or coworkers may leave; your company may be bought by another company; your job duties may change. When you get a new boss, you must prove yourself all over again. Be prepared for change, and stay aware of changes in the organizational culture.

Occasionally, you may find yourself in a dysfunctional work environment, or one that makes you uncomfortable or dissatisfied. First, work to adapt to the organizational culture, but don't let the culture bring you down. Get out and look for something that is a better fit for you.

Dress and Attitude

Act and dress in a style that is appropriate for your position and your institution. During your first few weeks on the job, dress conservatively— watch to see what others wear. People make snap judgments. Be yourself, but be your most practical, professional self. Let people get to know you before showing what an unusual person you are. Prove to your company that you understand them. Once you have established yourself as a professional who is in tune with the company or institution, you can begin to express your individuality. If you are interested in moving up in your institution, you may wish to dress more like those who have the positions you desire. For example, if you are an entry-level librarian at a library and you hope to be promoted to an administrative position at the same institution, you may wish to dress as the administrators do. This may help them visualize you in the position you want.

On your first job, some people may view you as immature or naïve. Stop thinking of yourself that way and it may help others stop viewing you that way. Find mentors, read literature, and express your interest in learning and contributing to the organization. Most organizations will be thrilled with your energy and new ideas. If your institution does not value the fresh perspective you bring to the organization, you may need to look for your second job, where people will view you as someone with experience, rather than someone fresh out of school.

Learn from Mistakes

Everyone makes mistakes. Don't overreact to your mistakes, but don't quit trying new things. Be sure you take initiative. "No one told me" won't work. Be honest if you make a mistake. Take responsibility for the error— never blame other people or external circumstances for your actions or decisions. Others, particularly those who report to you, will lose respect for you if you don't take the blame for something you did. Don't beat yourself up or dwell on your errors; admit your mistake and ask your supervisor or mentors how you can avoid repeating it. Use your mistakes as learning experiences and move on.

Work Ethics

Behave as if people are watching you every day. Just because everyone else is doing something wrong doesn't make it all right for you to do it. Use common sense when deciding whether something is ethical or not. If you're unsure, ask a colleague, mentor, or friend. Here are a few common sense "do's and don'ts," taken from *Rules of the Road: Surviving Your First Job Out of School.*

- Don't use company letterhead for personal business, complaint letters, résumés.
- Don't cheat on time sheets.
- Don't use the company phone for personal, long-distance calls.
- Find out your company's expectations about punctuality, flex time, and attendance. Some companies will allow more flexibility than others; be sure you have proven that you are accomplishing all your duties if taking advantage of a more flexible schedule.
- Don't send hasty angry e-mails or voice-mail messages. Wait twenty-four hours. Go home and write the message out and then delete it. In e-mail, say only "when can we talk?" or something neutral.
- Use caution when dealing with a company computer network. Don't send controversial mail through work e-mail. Don't download pornography or other nonwork-related files. Find out your company's policies and expectations for using the company's computers; some institutions will be more lenient than others. Remember that nothing you do on a company computer is really private; everything can be traced.
- Never say "it's not my job." If it really is someone else's job and you don't know how to do something, say "I think Susie usually does this, but I'll be glad to work with her on it" or something like that.

Time and Project Management

Develop time management skills. Set priorities and work on the most important or urgent projects first. Save the less-demanding projects or the enjoyable tasks for times when you are tired or when you are more likely to be interrupted. Try to develop a pattern for your workday. When are you most productive? When is it quieter in your area? Don't let yourself get too distracted by socializing, e-mailing, or surfing the Internet.

Develop project management skills. Again, set priorities—what is the most urgent project? Which projects will take the longest period of time? Which projects can be delegated or shared? When faced with a large or long-term project, break the project up into smaller tasks. List every step that you will need to take to accomplish that project. Then decide what steps or tasks need to be taken in what order. Set deadlines for each task. Post a list on your bulletin board, your computer, your daily planner, or someplace that will keep the list in front of you each day. Check off each task as you finish it. This will help keep you moving toward the goal and you will feel more productive as you see the tasks being marked off. This also helps you account for your time and the list of tasks will help you describe your accomplishments in performance reviews.

Try to close your door when you have to write or do a project that requires a great deal of concentration. Some workplaces don't allow you to do this— for example, if you are in a one-person library or work in a cubicle. If you don't have an office, develop strategies for working in an open area. Perhaps you can wear headphones to listen to music while you work, if this helps you concentrate. Perhaps you can adjust your work schedule so that you work when fewer people are in the area. If you are in a one-person library, you will have to work around interruptions. Try to work on projects requiring a great deal of concentration when you are more likely not to be interrupted—for example, perhaps fewer people use your library early in the morning. You may have to take some work home, particularly if you are trying to write, work on a long-term project, or work on professional committee assignments.

If you commit to a project, make sure you follow through with the project, and do it by the deadline promised. Keep your supervisor apprised of your progress and any problems you encounter. Don't force your supervisor to remind or nag you about deadlines. If you delegate tasks, always follow up to be sure arrangements are taken care of and that delegated work is being done. Take responsibility for tasks assigned to you, including things you delegate to others. If they do not accomplish their work, you are still ultimately responsible.

Running Effective Meetings

Learn to plan and run an effective meeting. You may be appointed to lead a committee or task force within your organization. If you do not have this opportunity, look for opportunities in professional or community organizations. Invite all participants to the meeting, giving them instructions about the date, time, place, and any information they should bring to the meeting. If necessary, remind them about the meeting a day or two before the meeting. Prepare and distribute a meeting agenda with the invitation or the reminder. Bring copies of the agenda and any supporting documentation to the meeting. When necessary, use parliamentary procedure to keep the meeting running smoothly and efficiently. Involve the group in the discussions, but keep the conversation on the topics assigned. Stay within the time allotted for the meeting; end the meeting on or before the time specified. Running an effective meeting is an often-overlooked skill that can make others respect your organizational skills, leadership abilities, and efficiency.

Handling Performance Reviews

Many institutions have scheduled annual performance reviews. To help prevent bad reviews, ask your supervisor about the review policy when you are hired. Get a blank review form. See what criteria are judged in your new company. It's difficult for your manager to remember what you have done during the past year. If possible, give him a list of accomplishments or a self-review before he does your performance evaluation. This helps your supervisor remember what you have done during the past year. Be honest about goals met and not met.

Don't be surprised if you have some surprises on your first review in a new job. You are learning the manager's perceptions, style, and expectations. Ask for more feedback if you don't understand something on the review. A good review should tell you bad and good things. A glowing review sometimes doesn't give you honest feedback. If your manager says you are perfect, ask how you can improve. This shows you are interested in growing. Set new goals with your manager.

If you get a bad review, don't get defensive or panic. Sometimes this is your fault; sometimes it's the manager's perception. When you understand that criticism is based on perception, you can change that view. Don't complain around work about a bad evaluation; this will brand you as a poor performer with a poor attitude. Blow off steam to nonwork friends who will be supportive. Talk with a mentor who may be able to give you constructive criticism or support or strategies for dealing with your manager.

If you do not have regularly scheduled performance reviews, ask your supervisor for feedback. Time your request carefully. If you ask at the wrong time, she may think you are too needy when things are difficult. Wait until a big project is over or until things are calmer. Ask for a chance to discuss "how you can improve next time." Give your manager time to think about what she wants to say. If you feel your coworkers seem to be avoiding you, make an appointment with your manager to find out if she has concerns about your performance. When you ask for feedback, be prepared to hear it. Don't get defensive. Listen to what your supervisor says. Don't argue, even if you think she is wrong. Remain calm, even if you don't like what you hear. Ask for time to think over what you have heard so you can discuss it when you are calmer.

If you are going to ask for a raise, be certain you can make your case. Don't ask for a raise immediately after a layoff; you are just lucky to have kept your job. Wait three months, and during that time, show that you are doing more than you were before.

Stress Management

Learn to prioritize and manage stress. It's all right to panic about a huge workload or a new assignment. Go ahead and panic—and then start prioritizing. Run your list of steps or priorities by someone else (perhaps your manager) to be sure you're on track. This helps you not duplicate work already being done by someone else. Then start working your way down the list. Your manager will want to see results, not just a lot of activity.

If you believe you need help, have a detailed list with you when you ask for reinforcements. Be able to back up your request. If you can't get help, think about untapped resources. Be creative; who else can help you get things done? Streamline whatever you can.

Be nice to yourself. Take some time to destress when you get home. Investigate stress management classes or other activities that can relieve your work-related stress.

Get a life outside of work. Don't make work your whole life. A good rule is to have three different things going on in your life—work, relationships, and hobbies; work, school, and volunteerism; and so on. Balance your life so that you don't get burned out. Develop hobbies or interests outside of librarianship. If you're lucky enough to love your job and your coworkers, it can be more difficult to separate your personal life from your work life. Still, try not to let your whole life to revolve around your work because if something goes wrong at work, your whole life is affected. If you have other circles of friends and activities, you have a release mechanism whenever you are feeling too stressed at work.

Ann Snoeyenbos described how she separates her professional life from her personal life. "My reasons for separating work and social life may not apply to other people, but because I work and live in the same neighborhood, and actually have colleagues living in the same building I do, it is vital for me to maintain emotional distance between the two. Otherwise it would feel like I was in college again, where perpetual guilt ruins your free time. Because your desk, your books, and the library are all so close, you feel like you should be studying constantly. But that just isn't realistic. If I have work to do outside of my regular work hours, I go to my office; I don't take it home with me.

"The other reason is that I have pretty strong sports commitments outside of work, but I don't want there to be any doubt in my boss's mind or my colleagues' minds that I am committed to my job. I don't want them ever to be able to say 'your sport seems to be interfering in your work,' and to make sure of that, I never talk about that part of my life while I'm at work. In fact, at work I talk almost not at all about the things I do outside of work. It simply isn't my colleagues' business, but if they did know it could possibly come back to haunt me (indirectly or directly) in a performance review. I do talk about my Book Club at work," clarified Snoeyenbos, "because that is almost a job-related activity."

EDUCATION

In library school, take a wide variety of subjects. You never know what will be useful. Take at least one cataloging course and one reference course, even if you are convinced that you won't need them. You will. If possible, take a financial management course and a technology course. Most experts recommend taking a variety of subjects to see what you may enjoy. You never know what your job may require of you, or what type of job you may hold ten years from the time you graduate. A broad perspective helps you see what options you may have. If you work in a small library, such as a one-person special library, you will have to do everything. If you work in a large library or in the private sector, your job will change over time and you will find a variety of knowledge very helpful.

Will Olmstadt (librarian, Medical Sciences Library, Texas A&M University) said, "From personal experience, I purposely did an intensive cataloging and authority control internship, in addition to taking the introductory course, while in my MLS program. While I'm now employed in a public services position, this solid cataloging background was one of my most highly regarded traits during interviews. I don't regret a minute of it. Making my experience as broad as possible was one of the smartest moves I ever made."

"I hated cataloging class," laughed Anne Haines (collections reference assistant, Indiana University), "but understanding the system has really helped me in my support staff position, and will be very useful as I move on in my career. I'd also recommend the converse—take a reference class even if you want to be a cataloger—not only will you gain a better understanding of user needs (ultimately, library users are a large part of the reason why all librarians do what they do, even if they never conduct a reference interview in their lives) but it will give you research skills like you wouldn't believe! And if you ever want to publish or do research (if you end up in an academic library, you'll probably have to), you'll be very grateful for the skills gained in a reference class."

Additional Formal Education

Many people come into librarianship after being in another field. If you already have a master's degree in another area, you are well positioned for many academic library or special library jobs. If you do not have a second master's degree, consider a second degree or some further education. Academic library jobs often require or prefer a second master's in a subject area. You might start working on a second degree the minute you land your first professional job, although many people wish to wait a year or two to get settled in their first position. Find out what is common among the people who hold your ideal job—for example, do you need a Ph.D.? An MBA? A subject specialty? Consider what subject might be helpful—for example, an MBA gives you an edge as a manager, because you will have management, marketing, accounting, financial management, and personnel skills that someone without your education will not have. Investigate any education benefits offered by your employer—for example, many academic institutions offer a tuition waiver for employees to take one course per semester.

Recognize the time commitment that is involved in pursuing a second degree while working full-time. Talk with your supervisor before beginning a program. Don't do your schoolwork while you are at your job, unless your employer encourages you to do so. Don't let your course load interfere with your attendance or performance at work. Don't expect special treatment (for example, not working a night shift if all other reference librarians do so) because you are in school.

Continuing Education

Attend workshops or educational opportunities that can help you develop and learn new skills. For example, medical librarians can earn continuing education credits that can result in accreditation. Special libraries and corporations often fund professional development very highly. Institutional funding varies wildly, so ask about professional development support when you interview at an organization.

Most professional associations hold conferences and often offer other continuing education opportunities. Check the Web sites, newsletters, or magazines of any professional association, such as the American Library Association, to find out what workshops or conferences may interest you. Find out which workshops, training sessions, or conferences have been most helpful to your colleagues and those in your desired field. Determine what skills you would like to learn, either to improve your performance on your current job or prepare you for the job you wish to obtain in the future. Find out which conferences allow you to make contact with those in the field you wish to investigate or enter. You will often have to spend some of your own money to do this, but view it as an investment in your future. Investigate grants and other forms of funding for conferences. Try to locate meetings closer to home, such as state or regional conferences. Also, look into Web-based training or other inexpensive options.

Self Education

Develop expertise in specific knowledge areas that will help you get your dream job. Read a variety of literature in and outside the field, to stay up to date on trends in the information field and trends that affect our field and our world.

There is little job security and job loyalty anymore. Develop a sense of loyalty to your career. Make sure you give your company what they need so that you can get the training and experience you need to move on, even if moving on means moving to a new organization. Take advantage of job training and seminars. Make sure you leave smarter than you started. If the company lays others off, or people leave your organization, that might offer you an opportunity for you to restructure your job to gain new skills.

MARKET YOURSELF

If you're in a tenure track situation, you will be expected to keep a file of your accomplishments documenting your progress. In whatever type of job you are in, keep a file of what you've done that year. Keep things like handouts or memos or presentations you have produced, letters of commendation or thanks, samples of work, articles, anything documenting your accomplishments. Use this in your annual review process to remind yourself and your supervisor what you've done that year. Use it when you write your résumé or perhaps in your interview. Keep it for future reference; sometimes ideas can be generated from earlier ideas. These files also give you perspective on what you've done throughout your career.

Once you get one job, you should start preparing for your next job (within or outside of the company you're presently working for). Watch the job ads and see what kind of experience is being required. Use your work situation, professional involvement, and volunteer involvement to build the skills you will need to meet the criteria for your ideal job. For example, would budgeting experience help you land a management position? Do you need supervisory experience? Would learning a second language or earning a second master's degree help you get your ideal job? Use the time you have on this job to gain experience and skills needed for your next step. Look at people who have jobs that you want; what skills do they have? Talk to them and learn about their type of work. Don't get complacent; look for new things to do in your present job. If you can show that you improved your workplace in some tangible ways, that will be great for your résumé. It also continues to challenge you.

Getting promoted takes patience. Use your time to develop new skills and be sure to write down what you are accomplishing. Sometimes you can create a new job for yourself. Find something that really needs to be done, something that people complain about not getting done, and just start doing it. Once you start doing it, it will become more and more necessary—people would miss it if it weren't done. This will add more work to your life. Be sure you continue doing your assigned job well. Then you can make a case that you are really doing two jobs and you should be promoted into the new one. If not, you are well situated to look for a new job using your new skills.

Be sure to let people around you know what you're doing. Keep a file of accomplishments and let supervisors, coworkers, and professional contacts know (in a modest way, of course) what you're doing. This keeps your name in the top of their mind and associates you in their mind as someone who does things. Some hardworking but shy people can have trouble moving up because they are too modest to promote themselves. Their supervisors and contacts just don't know what they do.

Be careful, though—don't take "marketing yourself" so seriously that you alienate others. Don't brag about how much you are doing; don't become arrogant. Don't complain about how hard you work; don't become a martyr. Don't take credit for others' work. Don't start thinking you do more than others. Be honest and humble, but be aware that you are responsible for letting key people, such as your supervisor, know what you're doing. Have documentation of your accomplishments, or produce something that shows that you're a productive employee. Don't let people wonder what you do all day. Don't take yourself too seriously. Enjoy the new experiences that come your way.

THERE ARE NO FACTS, ONLY INTERPRETATIONS: AN ESSAY

by Jill Emery
Director, Electronic Resources Program, University of Houston

There is no typical day in the library anymore. There has not been a typical day in a library since the first major computer network switches were thrown on. By 1990, all the typical days had disappeared into the recesses of the dusty corners of the shambles of the shelf lists. The writing is no longer within the walls but projected out from them and librarians can't or don't look back.

So, what does that mean to you, a newly minted professional, standing at the cusp of this newly rising day? Your inheritance is a profession in crisis, littered with more minefields than Bosnia. There are the tenure issues, the .com competition, and the slow bleeding off of decent benefits packages. There are no specific answers; your work-life will be more subjective and tentative. Your days will evolve into fending off one crisis or another, you'll move from one team project to another, you'll be on more committees than you thought possible. You have two paths to choose from—you can see this career as a funhouse or else, as a house of horrors. Either way, the future is tricky and the following advice is a condensed vision of many voices that have guided me to this point in my library career.

   1. *Become a Listener*: Learn the fine art of listening to others—all others, not just patrons. You can learn invaluable amounts of information from various people both within and without the library community.

Listen to what people say when they find out you're a librarian, listen to what they praise, what they deride. Listen closely to faculty, community leaders, teachers, and learn from them. Listen to bookstore clerks and to your government officials, listen to the world around you, and you will become a better librarian. Become a sounding board for people. Let them come to you when they are troubled, frustrated, or confused and listen. Use what you learn from these sessions to better serve your library, career, your daily activities.

2. *Accept Change*: It is the constancy of the life we now live. Things move from one format to another. You must move from one job to another to advance to the next professional level, and most often this movement will not occur in the same institution/library/city in which you currently dwell. Be willing to change and show your supervisors you are capable of initiating change. Change your screen saver and your PC wallpaper weekly. Change your hair color quarterly.

3. *Look for a Job with Autonomy*: The worst possible scenario you can find yourself in is having a domineering and overbearing boss. When searching for a job, look for one that allows you to make decisions, to voice an opinion, and to work both in teams and separate from them. However, for your first job, try to find a position that provides you with at least one strong role model. Seek out jobs at places where you know and respect your colleagues.

4. *Hide Your Insecurity*: Librarians, as a profession, are insecure and unfortunately, most of us show it too often. Work daily, hourly, to overcome your fears and insecurities. This is an insecure time, a new millennium, of frenetic technological change, evolving workplace paradigms. It is normal to be frightened by the complex social upheaval that is occurring, but do not project this fear. Find ways to handle the pressures of today's world and do not cause frequent scenes at work. It is, after all, only a job.

5. *Never Take Anything Personally*: This is a job. Your work is to be critiqued. Sometimes people will not like the job you do. Learn from the situation and move on. Do not allow anyone to make remarks about you personally. If you are criticized personally, ask the person what they mean by their remarks or by their statements.

6. *Learn to Project Slogans but Don't Adopt Any*: Everybody has a slogan these days. It's the way of the Web. Learn to use slogans adroitly but also learn not to adopt any one slogan outright. Mix and muddle your metaphors during presentations, in papers, and in

normal contexts of conversation. Do not allow yourself to be linked to any one concept or philosophy.

7. *Avoid Labels*: Do not let anyone label you. If you must wear a nametag at work, change the label on it weekly. Do not allow yourself to be pinned down in any way because you'll be seen only in that one way for the rest of your tenure in that job. Worse yet is to be labeled in professional arenas. Do not gain a reputation. Speak in public forums but change your message from one meeting to the next. Always ask questions but never, ever, make statements.

8. *Learn to Schmooze and Booze*: This is a highly social profession. Numerous social activities come with your job, so learn how to act at functions. Compliment people sincerely and never gossip. Drinking is not a necessity, but if you do drink, do not overdo it. Know your limits and do not exceed them at conferences. If you do overindulge, remove yourself promptly from the party or gathering.

9. *Maintain a Sense of Humor*: This is of utmost importance. If you cannot laugh at the situation you are in, then you've chosen the wrong profession. Academia is by and large a product of bureaucracy and as such an entity, you will find yourself doing the same thing over and over and over and over again in slightly different ways to appease people in slightly different jobs. Send out a joke once a week to your colleagues. Always bear in mind who can take a joke and who cannot. Humor can backfire if used inappropriately or in the wrong context.

10. *Don't Be Afraid to Walk Away*: This profession is not for everyone. To be a librarian, you have to be capable of retaining and regurgitating vast amounts of information from various resources. You have to have the intelligence to connect facts and/or situations together into an overarching worldview. You have to anticipate where and when the next push technology will come from and what impact it will have on your library, your institution, and your life. Learn what your boundaries are as a person and when you've had enough. The skills you learn in this profession are highly marketable and can be represented in a myriad of ways. Do not be afraid to get frustrated enough to quit.

SUMMARY

- Get diverse experience at school, at work, and through professional involvement.
- Watch the organizational culture.

- Dress and act professionally, and adapt your behavior to the culture of the organization.
- Learn from your mistakes.
- Learn to manage your time and your projects.
- Follow through on your commitments.
- Learn to run effective meetings.
- Learn from performance reviews.
- Learn to manage stress.
- Get a broad education in library school, and continue diversifying your education through further formal or continuing education opportunities.
- Continue to educate yourself by keeping up with professional literature.
- Market yourself.
- Keep files to document your accomplishments.
- Don't take yourself too seriously.
- Be prepared for constant change.

RELATED READINGS

Experience

Luppert, Eve. *Rules for the Road: Surviving Your First Job Out of School*. New York: Berkley Publishing, 1998.

Tye, Joe, with National Business Employment Weekly. *Personal Best: 1001 Great Ideas for Achieving Success in Your Career*. New York: John Wiley, 1997.

Wallace, Virginia L. "A Word to the Wise (and Often Weary): Advice for a New Librarian." *The School Librarian's Workshop* 12 (June 1992): 13–14.

Organizational Culture

Budd, John. "The Organizational Culture of the Research University: Implications for LIS Education." *Journal of Education for Library and Information Science* 37 (spring 1996): 154–62.

Edwards, Catherine E. "Change and Conflict in the Academic Library." *Library Management* 21, no. 1 (2000): 35–41.

Jurow, Susan Rachel. "Using Consultants to Build a More Creative Organizational Culture." In *Using Consultants in Libraries and Information Center: A Management Handbook*, edited by Edward Dale Garten. Westport, Conn.: Greenwood Press, 1992.

Richards, Robert C. "Biz of Acq—Stewardship, Partnership, Self-Understanding: An Exploration of Values in Acquisitions Work." *Against the Grain* 12, no. 3 (June 2000): 87–90.

Rosenqvist, Kerstin. "Work Ethics and Professionalism." *Scandinavian Public Library Quarterly* 21, no. 4 (1988): 4–8.

Sannwald, William W. "Understanding Organizational Culture." *Library Administration & Management* 14, no. 1 (winter 2000): 8–14.

Shaughnessy, Thomas. "Organizational Culture in Libraries: Some Management Perspectives." *Journal of Library Administration* 9, no. 3 (1988): 5–10.

Project Management

Anzalone, Filippa Marullo. "Project Management: A Technique for Coping with Change." *Law Library Journal* 92 no. 1 (winter 2000): 53–70.

Bell, Suzette. "Keeping the Plates Spinning." *Library Association Record* 98 (August 96): 412–13.

Chambers, Shirley. "Introducing Project Management Techniques to the Robinson Library, University of Newcastle." *Journal of Librarianship and Information Science* 30, no. 4 (December 1998): 249–58.

White, Robert L. "Project Management: an Effective Problem-Solving Approach." In *Advances in Library Administration and Organization* 2 (1983).

Time Management

Bacon, Pamela S. "Quit Playing Catch-Up." *School Library Journal* 45, no. 6 (June 2000): 35.

Cennamo, Katherine Sears. "You Want It When??? Time Management Tools for Media Production Centers." *Ohio Media Spectrum* 43 (summer 1991): 25–9.

Cochran, J. Wesley. *Time Management Handbook for Librarians.* Westport, Conn.: Greenwood Press, 1991.

Cox, Robin Overby. "River of Time: Rethinking and Renewing Library Stewardship." *Library Administration & Management* 14, no. 4 (fall 2000): 209–17.

DeFord, Vicki. "Time Management." *The Unabashed Librarian*, no. 104 (1997): 14–16.

Dysart, Jane I. "Ten Commandments of Good Time Management." *PNLA Quarterly* 55 (winter 1991): 17–18.

Foust, J'aime. "Dewey Need to Be Organized?" *Book Report* 19, no. 2 (September/October 2000): 20–3.

Gothberg, Helen M. "Time Management in Public Libraries: A Study of Public Libraries." *Public Libraries* 30 (November/December 1991): 350–7.

———. "Time Management in Special Libraries." *Special Libraries* 82 (spring 1991): 119–29.

———. "Time Management in State Libraries." *Special Libraries* 82 (fall 1991): 257–66.

Jasper, Richard P. "Paying Peter Back: Managing the Time for Collection Management." In *Acquisitions '90*, edited by David C. Genaway. Canfield, Ohio: Genaway, 1990.

Jenda, Claudine Arnold. "Management of Professional Time and Multiple Responsibilities in a Subject-Centered Academic Library." *Library Administration & Management* 8 (spring 1994): 97–108.

Kohl, David F. "Had We But World Enough, and Time . . ." *Collection Management* 22, no. 1–2 (1997): 43–55.

Nauman, Ann Keith. *Making Every Minute Count: Time Management for Librarians*. Library Learning Resources, 1991.

Nofsinger, Mary M. "Time Management Skills: A Checklist." *College & Research Libraries News*, no. 10 (November 1996): 648–50.

Pandora, Cherie Pettit. "Time Management for the Overworked, Understaffed, Library/Media Specialist." *Ohio Media Spectrum* 44 (fall 1992): 67–70.

Proctor, Sandra J. "Time Management in Law Firm Libraries." Thesis, University of North Carolina at Chapel Hill, 1993.

Tumlin, Markel D. "Time Management Considerations for Balancing Optical Disc Point-of-Use Instruction with Other Reference Services." *Microcomputers for Information Management* 10 (September 1993): 215–26.

Watkins, Denise M. "Are You a Time Management Junkie?" *Information Outlook* 3, no. 1 (January 1999): 34–5.

Yucht, Alice H. "Mailbox Methodology." *Book Report* 12 (September/October 1993): 13.

Running Meetings

Fellows, Mary. "Conducting Effective Meetings." In *Youth Services Librarians as Managers*, edited by Kathleen Staerkel. Chicago, Ill.: American Library Association, 1995

McCallister, Myrna Joy. "Conducting Effective Meetings." In *Practical Help for New Supervisors*, edited by Joan Giesecke. Chicago, Ill.: American Library Association, 1997.

Stress Management

Grosser, Kerry. "Stress and Stress Management: A Literature Review." *LASIE* 15 (March/April 1985): 2–24.

Hudson, Mary Pelzer. "Conflict and Stress in Times of Change." *Library Management* 20, no. 1 (1999): 35–8.

Ollendorff, Monica A. "How Much Do Librarians Know about Stress Management?" *Behavioral & Social Sciences Librarian* 8, no. 1–2 (1989): 67–98.

"Stress Management Techniques." *The Unabashed Librarian* no. 102 (1997): 8.

Wolcott, Mary. "Stress Management." *Indiana Media Journal* 7 (summer 1985): 15–18.

Education

De Cagna, Jeff. "Learning is a Matter of Principle: Part 1." *Information Outlook* 4, no. 4 (April 2000): 10.

———. "Nurturing Our Genuine Commitment to Learning." *Information Outlook* 4, no. 5 (May 2000): 14–15

Van Riel, Rachel. "Training the Librarians of the Future." *Public Library Journal* 14, no. 3 (autumn 1999): 58–9.

Continuing Education

Abell, Angela. "New Roles? New Skills? New People? (Continuing Professional Development and Librarians)." *Library Association Record* 99, no. 10 (October 1997): 538–9.

Clarke, Zoe. "Help in the Early Years (Library and Information Studies Training Network (LISTEN); Professional Development Seminars for Young Librarians)." *Library Association Record* 100, no. 11 (November 1998): 591.

Farmer, Jane C., and Fiona C. B. Campbell "Information Professionals, CPD and Transferable Skills (Study of Continuing Professional Development)." *Library Management* 18, no. 3–4 (1997): 129–34.

Farmer, Lesley S. Johnson. "The Many Paths to Professional Development." *Book Report* 13 (November/December 1994): 11.

Foster, Constance L. "The Professional Growth of Librarians: Small Steps and Giant Leaps in Providing Information Services." *Kentucky Libraries* 63, no. 3 (fall 1999): 4–7.

Gibbons, Andrew. "Take a Lesson from a Toddler (Learning Skills for Continuing Professional Development)." *Library Association Record* 99, no. 10 (October 1997): 548–9.

Ginsburg, Carol Linda. "Looking Ahead for Professional Development (for Members of SLA)." *Information Outlook* 2 no. 1 (January 1998): 39.

Grealy, Deborah S. "Lifelong Learning for Librarians: A Strategic Competency for White-Water Navigation." *Colorado Libraries* 26, no. 2 (summer 2000): 6–7.

Kenney, Donald J., and Gail McMillan. "State Library Associations: How Well Do They Support Professional Development? (Survey of 41 Association Presidents)." *RQ* 31 (spring 1992): 377–86.

Kigongo-Bukenya, Isaac M. N. "New Trends in Library and Information Fields and the Implications for Continuing Education." *Journal of Librarianship and Information Science* 31, no. 2 (June 1999): 93–9.

Lathrop, Lori. "Professional Development." *Key Words* 7, no. 1 (January/February 1999): 4–5.

Lenox, Mary F. "Nurturing Your Professional Development (Presented at the 1989 SLA Conference)." *Special Libraries* 81 (fall 1990): 360–4.

Locke, Joanne. "Staff Training and Development—An Expressed Need." *Education Libraries* 23, no. 2–3 (1999): 7–8.

McElroy, Rennie. "Continuing Professional Development: Towards a Strategy and a Structure." In *The Education and Training of Information Professionals*; ed. by G.E. Gorman Lanham, Md.: Scarecrow Press, 1990.

Miller, Susan J. "Professional Development for the Library Media Specialist." *Book Report* 17, no. 5 (March/April 1999): 20–1.

Monty, Vivienne I., and Peggy Warren-Wenk. "Using the Internet As a Professional Development Tool: An Analysis." *Education Libraries* 18 (spring 1994): 7–10.

Nankivell, Clare. "Have You Been Framed? (Use of the Library Association's Framework for Continuing Professional Development)." *Library Association Record* 99, no. 10 (October 1997): 553–4.

Paul, Karin. "Professional Development: It's Good for Your Soul." *School Libraries in Canada* 13 (fall 1993): 2.

"Professional Development: and Tomorrow—the World." *Library Association Record* 102, no. 2 (February 2000): 67.

Reid, Marion T. "Professional Development: Then and Now." *Florida Libraries* 41, no. 6 (September/October 1998): 127–8.

Roper, Fred W. "MLA's Professional Development Program: How We Took Control of Our Future." *Bulletin of the Medical Library Association* 86, no. 2 (April 1998): 211–6.

Scott Cree, John. "Professional Development: A Bluffer's Guide." *Catalogue & Index*, no. 132 (summer 1999): 8–10.

Swaffield, Laura. "How the Others Stay on Top (Comparing Continuing Professional Development in Different Professions)." *Library Association Record* 99, no. 10 (October 1997): 536–7.

Varlejs, Jana. "Continuing Education by the Numbers." *Journal of Education for Library and Information Science* 40, no. 4 (fall 1999): 296–8.

———. "The Continuing Professional Education Role of ASIS: Fifty Years of Learning Together, Reaching Out, Seeking Identity." *Journal of the American Society for Information Science* 50, no. 11 (September 1999): 1032–6.

Wade, Anne. "Resources on the Net: Professional Development." *Education Libraries* 23, no. 2–3 (1999): 35–7.

Weingand, Darlene E. "Continuing Professional Education: Luxury or Necessity?" *Journal of Education for Library and Information Science* 39, no. 4 (fall 1998): 332–3.

———. "Describing the Elephant: What Is Continuing Professional Education?" *IFLA Journal* 26, no. 3 (2000): 198–202.

Wetherbee, Louella Vine. "Staff Development As a Component of Organizational Renewal." *Texas Library Journal* 75, no. 1 (spring 1999): 24–7.

Self Education

Varlejs, Jana. "On Their Own: Librarians' Self-Directed, Work-Related Learning." *The Library Quarterly* 69, no. 2 (April 1999): 173–201.

CHAPTER 4

Networking

The key to this business is personal relationships.

—Dicky Fox, *Jerry Maguire* (1996)

Why should you network? Networks provide information, support, development, and influence. You develop your network of experts—people who know things, or people you can go to for certain types of information. Some network contacts offer support by offering moral support or practical help. Mentors and experts in your network can help further your professional development and training. Networks can help enhance your influence and visibility, and can open doors for your career. Your contacts can support your current position by offering you feedback, training, problem solving, and benchmarking. Contacts can offer recommendations or serve as references. They can also help you widen your personal circle of friends.

Networking helps your career in many ways. Networks can facilitate your career by offering assistance, giving early warning of situations or trends, and providing influence in certain circles. Contacts can alert you to job openings, can serve as references, and can put in a good word for you at their organization. They can speak about their personal knowledge of you, particularly if they have seen you produce and interact in a committee or professional situation.

"Networking has helped me in day-to-day problem solving," said Laura Sill. "I not only have local colleagues to consult, but colleagues from around the world. Networking has provided me with potential job offers and with opportunities in professional organizations such as the American Library Association (ALA). Professional involvement has broadened my view of issues I deal with day to day. In other words, I don't generally take a local view of questions, problems, or issues. I tend to think big picture, and I would say this is in part because I am able to be professionally involved. It provides perspective."

Ann Ercelawn agreed. "Professional involvement expands our world of colleagues and our perspectives, as well as enhancing skills, whether or not it leads to career advancement—though it usually does. Professional involvement in the North American Serials Interest Group (NASIG) has kept me from 'plateauing' out years ago, by providing me many more opportunities to learn new skills than I have in my local environment. I've learned how to manage electronic discussion lists, how to create Web pages, how good committees work, and many other things from my involvement with NASIG. Best of all, I have a large network of colleagues to call upon for assistance or advice in all sorts of areas because I know them through professional associations."

"I do professional editing," explained Wayne Jones. "Networking helps me establish contacts with people whom I can then ask to contribute to books or special volumes that I am editing. I have gained assurance from working with committees, as I have discovered that I often do know more about a subject than I had realized."

WHAT IS NETWORKING?

The term "networking" sometimes has bad connotations. Some people think it sounds as if they are using other people, or as if they are being insincere. On the contrary, networking is all about developing relationships. What you need or get from a network may be different for everyone. For some, it's a structured, conscious effort; for others, it's as simple as getting support when you're having a bad day at work. Ideally, networking should be a give-and-take relationship—a friendship or a professional relationship you build with others. Networking can be about knowing the right people who can help you succeed.

There are three basic types of networks:

- Personal—family, friends, school friends, work friends, recreational friends, volunteer work, hobbies, sports, education, family, family's friends
- Organizational—boss, coworkers, project groups, committees
- Professional—associations, organizations, associates, colleagues, clients, peers, bosses, suppliers, vendors, past colleagues, alumni groups, competitors, electronic discussion lists, family, friends

HOW DO I NETWORK?

First, ask yourself: What do I want from my network? Is my current network serving me? How could my network work better for me? Then consider how you are already networking, perhaps without even realizing it.
  Do you:

- Usually accept opportunities to meet new people?
- Have contacts in a wide variety of groups?
- Feel that you're generally well informed?
- Share information with those around you?
- Stay in regular contact with your colleagues or clients?
- Regularly attend meetings, training courses, and conferences?
- Know and talk with peers in other organizations?
- Subscribe to and participate in electronic discussion lists?

If you answered "no" to any of the questions above, ask yourself . . . what prevents you?
  Your networking style may be influenced by your family's networks and networking approach. If you're shy, you can still network effectively. Camila Alire (director, Colorado State University Libraries) encouraged, "You don't have to be gregarious to be a good networker or leader. Many library leaders are somewhat reserved but are great leaders." Think of networking as building relationships. Maintain contact with people you meet at various jobs, school, conferences, and committee work, and soon, your network will grow.

Involvement in Professional or Community Associations

"Getting involved with one of the professional organizations is probably the most significant contribution you can make to your own career," wrote Sheila Pantry and Peter Griffiths in their book, *Your Successful LIS Career: Planning Your Career, CVs, Interviews, and Self-Promotion.* How do you get involved in a professional organization?
  Join an organization so that you'll receive their publications. Reading professional literature will help you learn the terminology and key players in the field, and keep up with current trends. Scope out the various organizations by talking with friends and colleagues and reading the association's

publications. Which ones will help you learn skills and meet people in the type of work you want to do? Which organization is the right "fit" for you? Table 4.1 lists a few guides to various library organizations. Nesbeitt and Gordon's book, *The Information Professional's Guide to Career Development Online*, includes a detailed list of many professional associations.

Once you are a member of an organization, volunteer for involvement in committees. If you are wondering how to start becoming involved in professional organizations, you might consider the American Library Association New Members Round Table. ALA NMRT guarantees a committee appointment to all volunteers in order to provide leadership development opportunities and a welcoming introduction to association involvement. Several state library associations also have an NMRT. Often, it's easier to get involved in a regional, state, or more specialized group initially, as those groups are smaller than national associations. Many people try several organizations to find the one that best fits their interests and needs. Also, your interests will change over time, so it may be quite helpful to make contacts in various organizations so that you meet a wide variety of people. It may take longer to break into large organizations, but keep ap-

Table 4.1   On-line Networking Resources

Guides to Associations
Library Organizations and Associations   http://www.libraryHQ.com/orgs.html
ALA Divisions, Units and Governance   http://www.ala.org/alaorg/
ALA Affiliate Web Site Directory   http://www.ala.org/alaorg/affiliates/affiliates_home.html
State Library Associations (ALA Chapter Web Site Directory)   http://www.ala.org/cro/chapdir.html

Guides to Conferences

Conference Planning Calendar
    (ALA Listing of Library Associations and Religious Holidays)
    http://www.ala.org/cro/cal.html

Guides to Discussion Lists
Library-Oriented Lists and Electronic Serials   http://www.wrlc.org/liblists/
Library E-mail Lists and Newsgroups   http://www.itcompany.com/inforetriever/email.htm
Liszt   http://www.liszt.com/

plying. Attend committee or business meetings, programs, and social activities to become better known, and you will be remembered when officers make committee appointments.

Jim Walther (reference librarian, Brian Cave LLP) said, " If you want to be known at the local level, get involved in local level groups or be instrumental in city groups, which may not be library focused. Sometimes local chapters may be named the same as the national organizations, but sometimes there are local groups that are unofficial. First, get involved in your local or state organizations and then look to one or two national organizations. Some informal organizations don't even have a name—for example, in Washington, D.C., there is an informal group called the Franklin Square group, which is comprised of law librarians in a specific section of the city. These groups are often topical groups or social groups that attract others based on where you live or work. Depending on the city, these groups have an informal, social, topical focus, and allow you to share information with others. Local chapters or informal groups can give you excellent leadership and organizational opportunities for involvement."

When you're put on a committee, find out what is expected of you and do it. People who "come through" are noticed, remembered, and recommended to others. People who don't respond to e-mail or don't do what they're asked are also remembered. Take your committee responsibilities seriously; if you can't commit the time, explain your situation to the committee chair or your supervisor, and if necessary, resign from the committee. You don't want to be "dead weight" on the committee. However, do remember that everyone is as busy as you are, and others do understand that you are volunteering your time to help on this committee. Talk with your committee chair or supervising officer if you have concerns about the time you can devote to the committee—sometimes their expectations are much lower than yours! Find the level of activity and the balance of commitment that works best for you.

Use committee involvement—professional, community, workplace, institutional, and so on—to help you gain skills you wouldn't gain on the job. For instance, if you would like some budgeting experience, try to get on a committee that manages a budget for a program or project. If you're good with money, volunteer to be the treasurer of a local or professional group. If you enjoy writing or want to gain writing or publishing experience, look for committees that publish newsletters or other publications. Consider submitting an article to your group's newsletter. If you want to gain supervisory experience, volunteer to chair a committee or run for an office. Diversify your skills by participating in activities you can't perform on your daily job.

Fran Wilkinson commented, "Perhaps the best thing I ever did profession-ally was get involved with NASIG. I learned conference planning skills, ex-panded my organizational skills (which helps me every day), developed ideas for research and publication. Most importantly, I developed professional col-leagues and friends who have inspired me, given me advice and new ideas for all aspects of my work, written letters of support for my tenure and promotion, let me bounce ideas off of them, and sought my advice, which forced me to think in new and different ways."

Ask questions. Learn. Correspond with the chair or supervisor and other committee members. Contribute ideas. Do what you're asked to do. That's how your name gets remembered.

Julie Ann McDaniel (librarian, Community Hospital of Springfield) wrote, "I think one of the best pieces of advice I ever got came from Rose-mary DuMont, then dean of the School of Library Science at Kent State Uni-versity. She said that to get started in professional associations you should volunteer on the committees/interest groups/sections that no one else wants to be on. She suggested some social issues groups or groups associated with small user populations—prison libraries; disabled services; homebound ser-vices; etc.; or new groups that are just trying to get organized in a larger group. She pointed out that in most organizations it is much easier to "move up" within these smaller sections. It was easier (and faster) to get to a lead-ership position where you could move into a section of the organization that more closely met your interests. She also indicated that if you worked in a large organization, you were more likely to be able to get time off to attend meetings of the smaller group. If you tried to get active in a larger group, you might find that many of your coworkers wanted time off to attend the same meetings. By being active in a smaller group, you were less likely to have competition to be away from work to attend meetings.

"It was advice that worked for me. I volunteered in the Ohio Library As-sociation Disabled Services Interest Group, a group of about six active peo-ple. Within two years, I was chair of the interest group. (On my job, I had no connection with or responsibility for anything related to patrons with disabilities.) I was able to write an article for *Ohio Libraries* about library services for the disabled. I ran for the next higher level of office in OLA and was defeated. At about the same time, I was active in the just-forming Bibliographic Instruction Interest Group of the Academic Library Associa-tion of Ohio. Again, this was a group of about ten active people. I was co-ordinator of BI at Kent State at the time, so it meshed well with my job. Be-cause of my work in OLA and my job responsibilities, I was invited to two OLA conferences to talk about BI. I was nominated for treasurer of ALAO and won, and then nominated for president and won. I attribute all of this to the suggestion to start small where no one else wanted to be. Had I started in the reference section of OLA, where I wanted to be (and my job responsibilities made sense for me to be), I would have been an 'extra' for a long time and would not have been able to move up in two organizations.

"I have found professional association work to be very rewarding personally," continued McDaniel, "and beneficial to my patrons. My patrons are impressed when I can say, 'I think XYZ library can help us with that. Let me call their librarian and see.' It is even better when I can send my patron to XYZ library and tell them to ask for 'June Smith.' I wouldn't know about the strengths of XYZ library or June Smith, the librarian, without my exposure to them through professional organizations."

Don't discount experience or contacts gained at community or social activities or organizations. Sometimes these people can steer you toward job opportunities or can help you gain skills you want. Not only can you gain diverse experience, you may also gain friends who provide support, balance, and a different perspective than you may receive at your workplace.

Committee Involvement at Your Workplace

Volunteer for special projects or committees at work. Suppose that your library is planning a big function, or that there is a big task that needs to be done. Volunteer to participate or to head up that project, and then do a good job at it. This puts you in touch with people you may not work with every day, and it shows your coworkers how you function in teams or as a leader. You will come in contact with different people and this will expand your network.

In a new job, don't rush into trying to identify with the powerful people. Sit back and watch others. Who are the hubs in your organization? Who knows information? Who gets things done? Who receives financial support for their projects? Who eats and socializes together? Be careful about forming alliances too soon. Others will form perceptions of you based on whom you socialize with, so don't get sucked into a clique at work. Watch people to determine who gets things done, who is respected, and who knows what's going on. These people can help you establish your network so that you will know what's going on and be able to get things done. You don't necessarily have to be friends with everyone—just try to treat everyone with respect so that you are able to work with them to accomplish things.

Communicate openly. In some hierarchical organizations, communication is often stifled, so find out how you can stay in the loop to get your work done and know what's happening in the organization. If you are in a position to encourage open communication, do so. If you're a supervisor, share information with your employees openly. Keep your supervisor informed. Copy essential people when writing e-mails. Don't leave people out of conversations about things that will involve them.

Attend Professional Conferences

Attend conferences or local meetings to meet people in the field, hear lectures, learn about trends, see products or services in exhibit areas, and make contacts. Ask friends and colleagues which conferences they find most beneficial. See table 4.1 for a few guides to professional conferences and associations. At conferences, attend social events. Make conscious efforts to meet people and develop friends and contacts. Wear your name badge to all events, so that people can see your name and remember it later.

"I am a huge advocate of networking," wrote Jennifer Doyle. "My first job was a direct result of this. Another thing I took advantage of as a student was all the discounted memberships to professional organizations. I joined almost every possible organization, one of which was the Special Libraries Association. The local SLA hosted monthly informal lunches and I attended one of these the February before I graduated, mainly to hear 'real' librarians talk about their jobs and their concerns. During this lunch, I met the woman who would become my first boss. At the time, I didn't realize that she had a job opening; however, she had mentioned that one of her part-time staff members was going on maternity leave. I was in a student job that I really enjoyed, but was part time, so I e-mailed her after the lunch and asked if she was looking for a temporary replacement. She said no, but she was looking for a permanent replacement for the full-time reference librarian who had just announced her retirement. After a formal interview (which was much less nerve-wracking since we had already met), I was hired and began the job the day after graduation. Without my connections through SLA, this never would have happened."

At professional meetings, use the opportunity to meet and interact with others in the profession, professionally and socially. Networking often offers support and encouragement that you may not receive on your daily job. Many librarians have gained lifelong personal friends, as well as helpful professional contacts, through interactions at conferences.

"After receiving an upbeat e-mail concerning the American Library Association Midwinter Meeting from a librarian I don't even know, I began

discussing with my coworker how much I enjoy my profession and love going to ALA conferences," mused Terri Holston (librarian, Johnston Community College). "Even though I have only been to a few, those few have
made a great impact on me. Everyone is so nice at the conferences, very
willing to talk to you and share with you their experiences as a librarian.
Not often in my hometown do I run into other librarians who I can share
with . . . sometimes I even get odd looks because I choose librarianship as
a profession (you know those looks, too!) As we were discussing, the Blind
Melon song 'No Rain' came to mind. It was popular in the early 1990s. Do
you know it—or more importantly, do you know the video?" asked Holston. "In the video, a young girl dressed as a tap-dancing bumblebee tries
desperately to find her niche. Eventually she does in 'Bumblebee Land,' a
beautiful grassy area where other tap-dancing bumblebees frolic and play.
ALA conferences are my 'Bumblebee Land'."

Make Diverse Contacts

Develop relationships with people in all areas of the information profession. This broadens your circle of contacts and widens your perspective on
the field. These contacts can offer you insight about different career opportunities, too. Librarians should not forget that vendors are good contacts.
Some new librarians may be intimidated by vendors. Vendors can be indispensable contacts and mentors. They can provide training and answer questions about a product or service so that your boss doesn't know you didn't
know something. They can give you a different perspective on the library
field. They can help you solve problems at work. They can alert you to potential job opportunities in other libraries. Also, you might find you're interested in working for a vendor. Vendors should develop relationships with
librarians. Don't view them only as customers. Make relationships with people outside your own line of work.

"In selling, networking is essential," said Bob Schatz. "From it comes
advice from people who can show you how to be more effective, references
for new prospective sales, introductions to people who can offer you more
rewarding work. In business, as in life, you can't have too many friends.
Seeing yourself as part of a professional network is an essential element of
truly professional work. Professional involvement keeps me in touch with
the values that took me to library school in the first place. I think I am more
effective in serving libraries if I maintain a heightened understanding and
appreciation for the issues that surround librarianship."

Table 4.2   NEWLIB-L

NEWLIB-L is a discussion list for librarians new to the profession who wish to share experiences and discuss ideas, issues, trends, and problems faced by librarians in the early stages of their careers. However, this list is also of interest to those who are considering becoming librarians, and to those established in the profession who might wish to mentor newcomers. The list is currently open to all librarians—academic, public, special, etc.

To subscribe, please send a note to: listproc@usc.edu with the message: "subscribe newlib-l Your Name" (please do not put in the quotation marks into your message, and replace "Your Name" with your name as you wish it to appear).

If you have any questions about the list, send a note to listproc@usc.edu with the message, "info newlib-l."

Source: Scheiberg, Susan (head, Acquisitions and Serials, RAND Library). E-mail message to NMRT-L (7 January 1999)

Table 4.3   NewBreed Librarian

NewBreed Librarian is a bimonthly Web publication intended to foster a sense of community for those new to librarianship, whether in school or just out. It consists of a daily news Weblog and letters from our readers. Every two months, NewBreed Librarian offers a new issue with a feature article and interview, advice from Susu, and helpful tips for the more technical side of librarianship in our column TechTalk. New issues also highlight progressive librarians and other information professionals in the People section, advertising exciting and exemplary work.

NewBreed Librarian debuted February 1, 2001, and as it matures, we hope to develop a searchable database in the Jobs category and include samples of grad school admission essays, résumés, cover letters, etc. in Xtras. Most importantly, NewBreed aims to use the Web to build community and foster collaboration among librarians. We're molding the Networks section with this objective in mind. Finally, we want the Web site to reflect the diversity of work that librarians do and provide an accurate picture of what librarianship is all about.

The URL is: <http://www.newbreedlibrarian.org>.

Source: Benedicto, Juanita (reference librarian, University of Oregon). E-mail message to NMRT-L (2 February 2001).

Participate in Electronic Discussion Lists

Find the lists that relate most to your job, or to what you want to do. Some of the guides to electronic discussion lists in table 4.1 may help you find lists you might like to join. Tables 4.2 and 4.3 describe NEWLIB-L, a list for new librarians and students, and NewBreed Librarian, a new on-line community for librarians. Subscribe to a few electronic lists and "lurk" for awhile to learn who's who and what type of concerns are discussed. Participate, but be sure your posts are in keeping with the type of issues discussed on the list. You will find out key people in the areas that interest you; and they may recognize your name if they later see it on an application for a job, committee appointment, or scholarship.

Judy Albert said, "Contacts with friends and classmates from graduate school have been helpful to me in providing information to patrons. For example, a friend who now works for the National Archives and Records Administration provided me with contact information for a patron who wanted to locate a CIA document. I have also found electronic discussion lists to be very helpful, both for specific job-related information, and for keeping up with the profession in general."

Make Conscious Efforts to Meet People

At conferences, meetings, and other group interactions, introduce yourself to people—speakers, people sitting by you, etc. You never know whom you might meet. Carry business cards, if you have them. Reintroduce yourself to people and remind them of where you met them. This helps them immediately place you in context until they get to know you better.

Use other peoples' networks. Ask friends, colleagues, and mentors to introduce you to others. Tell them if there's a specific person you'd really like to meet. Ask yourself what people you'd like to meet. Think about how many steps they are away from you in your network. Do you know anyone who knows them? Ask that person to help you meet them, or write them yourself.

When you meet people whom you have wanted to meet or consciously have planned to meet, try to have key things about them rehearsed so that you will stick in their mind. For example, tell this person "I have read your articles with interest" or point to some mutual interest or mutual friend.

If you read an article or attend a presentation that interests you, write the author or presenter. Most likely, the author or presenter will be happy to hear that someone has read and enjoyed their article or their presentation. Sometimes you can start an informal communication with this person or develop a relationship if you are interested in the same subject areas.

Sarah Nesbeitt wrote, "Since 1998, I've been a reviewer for a publication called *Electronic Resources Review*, and had kept in touch with the editor there fairly regularly in addition to writing my reviews. He's a librarian at an academic library around thirty minutes from where I live, so we'd share stories about the local area, places to go, etc., as well as information about what was going on with our own libraries. When he decided to retire from his position as editor, he asked me if I was interested in taking over for him, and he put me in touch with the publisher. They agreed with his decision, and I worked out an agreement with them. I took over as of the April 2000 issue."

Follow Through

Building and maintaining a network takes effort and time. Try to remember people's names later. Remembering someone's name can make him or her appreciate and remember you. Write follow-up notes after conferences. For example, "It was very nice meeting you. I enjoyed your speech." Spell names correctly. Pay attention to nicknames used or disliked, if possible.

Once you have made contacts, prove yourself. The library world is a small one, and people talk. Be sure your actions are honest and you treat others with respect. Don't use people for your own gain. Don't treat people badly. Don't burn your bridges when leaving a job, or commit to committee work and not follow through, for example. People talk, and you may gain a reputation you hadn't anticipated.

"Networking is valuable in developing a career or moving up," said Camila Alire. "I doubt there's anyone who's a leader who's not a good networker. Most of the time, it just happens; you don't consciously network. You often realize as you prove yourself to someone that the person might be willing to nominate you or recommend you for something. Prove yourself through your work, committee work, volunteering; always follow through. Be out there! You can't network if you're not involved. Word gets around in our field. Prove yourself. As an example, I have a colleague who always knew she had to develop her network to advance. She knew that sometimes it's who you know. She worked with the state librarian and volunteered to be involved with the state librarian's projects. She overtly tried to meet people. Of course, she had to prove herself and follow through once she got these appointments. Through conscious networking, she met people who could attest to her abilities."

NURTURE YOUR NETWORK

Establish networks by keeping in touch, taking initiatives, gaining access to people, and cultivating contacts. Nurture networks by being open-minded, keeping commitments, treating others as you'd want to be treated, not being afraid to ask for information or help, giving and saying thank you. Be open-minded. Treat everyone the same, even if you think you don't like someone, because you don't know what they might have to offer you once you get to know them. Be honest. Integrity (or the lack of) will gain you a reputation. You don't want to use people and throw them away. Be genuine about enjoying meeting new people and making new friends. Be open to what people can teach you and what you can give them. Keeping commitments builds trust. Don't be too proud to ask for help or to admit you don't know how to do something. Saying thank you and being willing to give to others helps you gain friends who will help you and remember you later.

Networks evolve over time and change according to your interests. Contacts must be maintained, and occasionally they must be pruned. Reevaluate your networks from time to time. Sometimes you need to distance yourself from harmful people or people whose attitudes or reputations will damage your network. Sometimes you will realize that you are in a one-way relationship that is not helping you. Distance yourself from people who drain your energy and hurt your reputation.

Stay in contact with people. Keep them informed of what you're doing, and learn what they're doing. Consciously add to your network. Keep your goals in mind; try to participate in circles (committees, organizations, etc.) that allow you to meet people you want to meet. Thank people who have assisted you. Invest time and energy into your network. Soon you will have a circle of friends and colleagues who can help you navigate your career.

SUMMARY

- Recognize that developing relationships with others can provide support, guidance, job leads, and more.
- Get involved in professional or community organizations.
- Volunteer for committee involvement or interdepartmental projects at your workplace.
- Attend professional conferences.
- Make contacts in diverse areas of the information field and beyond.
- Participate in electronic discussion lists.
- Make conscious efforts to meet people.
- Follow through to prove yourself.
- Nurture your network, and weed it when necessary.

RELATED READING

Networking

Crosby, John H. "Networking the Right Way." *Information Outlook* 4, no. 8 (August 2000): 12.

Liangzhi, Yu. "Community Networking: Development, Potentials and Implications for Public Libraries." *Journal of Librarianship and Information Science* 31, no. 2 (June 1999): 71–83.

Michelli, Dena, and Alison Straw. *Successful Networking*. Hauppauge, N.Y.: Barron's Educational Series, 1997.

Moore, Richard K. "A First-Class Guide to Networking (with Other School Librarians)." *Journal (California School Library Association)* 21, no. 1 (fall 1997): 8–10.

Nesbeitt, Sarah, and Rachel Singer Gordon. *The Information Professional's Guide to Career Development Online*. Medford, N.J.: Information Today, 2001. Includes chapters on networking on-line and a comprehensive list of library association Web sites.

Rux, Paul Philip. "Practical Networking Lessons (Tips from an All-Day Workshop)." *Book Report* 16 (May/June 1997): 29.

Tullier, L. Michelle. *Networking for Everyone! Connecting with People for Career and Job Success*. Indianapolis, Ind.: JIST Works, 1998.

Professional Involvement

"ACRL Leadership Opportunities: Get Involved in Your Association." *College & Research Libraries News* 61, no. 9 (October 2000): 814–7.

Bobinski, George S. "Is the Library Profession Over-Organized?" *American Libraries* (October 2000): 58.

"Book Trade Associations, United States and Canada." In *The Bowker Annual Library and Book Trade Almanac 2000*, edited by Dave Bogart. New Providence, N.J.: R. R. Bowker, 2000.

Bourdon, Cathleen. "The Association's Associations: ASCLA: Small but Special!" *American Libraries* 31, no. 6 (June/July 2000): 10.

Dowling, Brendan. "The Association's Associations: PLA What's In It For You?" *American Libraries* 31, no. 9 (October 2000): 9.

Ford, Barbara J. "Voices and Visions: Ten Ways to Get Involved in ALA." *American Libraries* 28 (September 1997): 9.

Ford, Simon. "Networking: the Art of Conferencing." *Library Association Record* 100, no. 4 (April 1998): 194–5.

"Foreign Library Associations." In *The Bowker Annual Library and Book Trade Almanac 2000*, edited by Dave Bogart. New Providence, N.J.: R. R. Bowker, 2000.

Frank, Donald G. "Activity in Professional Associations: The Positive Difference in a Librarian's Career." *Library Trends* 46 no. 2 (fall 1997): 307–19.

Glendenning, Barbara J., and James C. Gordon. "Professional Associations: Promoting Leadership in a Career." *Library Trends* 46, no. 2 (fall 1997): 258.

Greiner, Joy M. "Professional Views: Reasons to Attend the 1991 PLA National Conference; Section Presidents' Views on Public Librarians' Involvement in Professional Organizations." *Public Libraries* 29 (September/October 1990): 265–70.

Horrocks, Norman. "ALA Committees: How to Get Involved . . . and Why." *School Library Journal* 35 (June 1989): 41–44.

"International and Foreign Book Trade Associations." In *The Bowker Annual Library and Book Trade Almanac 2000*, edited by Dave Bogart. New Providence, N.J.: R. R. Bowker, 2000

"International Library Associations." In *The Bowker Annual Library and Book Trade Almanac, 2000*, edited by Dave Bogart. New Providence, N.J.: R. R. Bowker, 2000.

Jenkins, Althea H. "Realities of Involvement in the Total Structure: Your Professional Associations." In *National Conference of African American Librarians*. Columbus, Ohio: Black Caucus of the American Library Association, 1992.

Johnson, Margaret Ann. "The Association's Associations: ALCTS Marks 100 Years." *American Libraries* 31, no. 3 (March 2000): 10.

Mertes, Kate. "Networking: The Real Reason to Go to the ASI National Conference." *Key Words* 7, no. 4 (July/August 1999): 25–6.

Mundell, Jacqueline. "The Association's Associations: LITA Builds on Success." *American Libraries* 31, no. 8 (September 2000): 10.

"National Library and Information-Industry Associations, United States and Canada." In *The Bowker Annual Library and Book Trade Almanac 2000*, edited by Dave Bogart. New Providence, N.J.: R. R. Bowker, 2000.

Singer, Rebecca. "The Association's Associations: ALSC Works for Young Readers." *American Libraries* 31, no. 4 (April 2000): 9.

"State, Provincial, and Regional Library Associations." In *The Bowker Annual Library and Book Trade Almanac 2000*, edited by Dave Bogart. New Providence, N.J.: R. R. Bowker, 2000

"State School Library Media Associations." In *The Bowker Annual Library and Book Trade Almanac 2000*, edited by Dave Bogart. New Providence, N.J.: R. R. Bowker, 2000.

"The State of State Library Associations." *Illinois Library Association Reporter* 18, no. 5 (October 2000): 11–13.

Sullivan, Maureen. "Leadership in the National Arena." *Texas Library Journal* 75, no. 4 (winter 1999): 140–1.

Waddle, Linda L. "The Association's Associations: YALSA Becomes Printz-Oriented." *American Libraries* 30, no. 11 (December 1999): 7.

Ward, Kerry. "The Association's Associations: ALTA is Home for Trustees, Advocates." *American Libraries* 31, no. 5 (May 2000): 10.

Wilt, Charles. "The Association's Associations: LAMA is on the Move." *American Libraries* 31, no. 7 (August 2000): 8.

CHAPTER 5

Interpersonal Skills

What we've got here is failure to communicate.

—Captain, *Cool Hand Luke* (1967)

What are interpersonal skills? The ability to communicate clearly and listen effectively . . . the ability to work with different types of people . . . the ability to work with difficult people. Although some people are born with more advanced interpersonal skills than others, these skills can be learned and certainly can be improved.

"Most job ads ask for 'good interpersonal skills,'" Camila Alire pointed out. "This is probably one of the most misunderstood areas for new librarians. When you're dealing with people, future employers want to know if you can work well in a team environment. I like to call them 'human relation skills.' Treat people the way they want to be treated, the way you want to be treated. If you advance because you have great technical skills but no people skills, you will have trouble going far. People can develop, and should work to develop, good interpersonal skills."

Interpersonal skills may be:

- Communication skills (oral, written, listening, speaking)
- Social skills
- Attitude
- Human interaction and people skills
- Styles of behavior (positive response and professional manner)
- Approachability and helpfulness
- Leadership and teamwork
- Understanding of different work styles and how to communicate with others

How can interpersonal skills help you? Strong interpersonal skills lead to great organizational development, better customer care, better teamwork, greater job satisfaction, united and cooperative efforts, more productive meetings, and more effective communication, persuasion, and diplomacy.

Bob Schatz said, "Interpersonal skills are everything in professional work, starting with your relationship with yourself. You have to believe that what you are doing has value, and that you are not being asked to represent things you do not believe. From that, you have to carry the same level of respect and commitment to the way in which you communicate and interact with coworkers, employees, and customers. Professional work should be a reflection of who you really are, not something you do only during the workday. Stress and failure at work are more a result of discontinuity than anything else. Good interpersonal skills help maintain a balance among competing emotions/demands. It is this balance that allows one to see problems as challenges, and not crushing defeats."

COMMUNICATION

Interpersonal relationships begin with genuine two-way communication. The communication process begins with the sender, who encodes a message, which is decoded by the receiver. Communication is made up of verbal, vocal, and visual elements. Verbal communication is the words we use. Vocal communication is our tone of voice, intensity, etc. Visual communication is the nonverbal, body language; this is the most important part of the process.

Everyone has a different communication style. Use the Myers-Briggs Type Indicator or a similar personality-typing instrument to figure out what type of worker and communicator the person is. Try to communicate with them in the way that best reaches them. For example, some people respond to direct, forceful, oral communication. Others respond better to an e-mail or memo followed by a quiet conversation.

Many common problems occur during communication. Errors can occur during sending—for example, the sender may use vague or incorrect words; or the message may be obscured or distorted by the speaker's tone of voice, gestures, or body language. People process and respond to the nonverbal and vocal elements before they can focus on the words you use. The speaker may have a heavy accent, use a monotone voice, say "um" regularly, or not make eye contact. Communication errors may occur during transmission due to environmental noise, such as the phone ringing or having the television on. Errors can occur on the receiver's end when the receiver is bored, inattentive, distracted, or preoccupied.

"One of my undergraduate majors was interpersonal communication, so I know how important communication can be, "said Fran Wilkinson. "I am finding that in my current position as a higher-level library administrator, everything I say seems to carry more weight. It is very important to choose the correct words or phrases when giving instructions or describing a situation. I also specify in what context I am communicating. For example, am I just brainstorming ideas as a library faculty member, or am I giving a directive as an administrator? In terms of getting things done, I feel that it is important for people to be informed and understand why something is being done as a priority and why something else may not be done or funded. In addition to the usual means of doing this, I have an open door policy and the dean and I hold monthly open forums at which anyone can sign up and ask questions of us—there is no set agenda, the time belongs to those who sign up."

Communication is a two-way street—listening is more important than communicating. "Listening is a manager's most important skill," wrote Tony Alessandra and Phil Hunsaker in their book *Communicating at Work*. Effective listening leads to improved relationships, fewer misunderstandings, better teamwork, and improved morale. Although we may think we are good listeners, there are many barriers to effective listening. Active listening is hard work. There are many distractions out there. We think we know what the person will say and we rush to take action or comment. There is a huge gap between our speed of listening (400–500 words per minute) and speaking (135–175 words per minute). A typical employee's listening effectiveness is about 25 percent. The untrained listener will remember about 50 percent of a conversation immediately afterward and about 25 percent several days later. In other words, we forget about three-quarters of what we have been told. Listening saves time and avoids misunderstandings.

Alessandra uses the CARESS acronym to outline a plan for effective listening.

- *Concentrate*. Focus attention on the speaker and try to eliminate distractions or noise. Barriers include environmental barriers such as noise in the room, uncomfortable room (for example, too hot or too cold), other people talking, visual distractions (such as people walking by), or physical disruptions (such as having the TV or radio on). Speaker-related barriers include the speaker's style of dress, mannerisms, body language, accent, or speaking style. Listener-related barriers include physical barriers, such as hunger, fatigue, pain, pressure, time constraints, or psychological barriers such as boredom, day-dreaming, close-mindedness, physical proximity to the speaker, personal values, past experiences, or future expectations. Try to create a quiet, distraction-free, neutral space to talk. Realize that some people are contact-oriented and others are not; try to accommodate the person's style. Try deep breathing to help you concentrate and resist the urge to interrupt. Consciously decide to listen. Paraphrase what the speaker is saying. Make eye contact.

- *Acknowledge.* Demonstrate interest and attention. Make eye contact. Use verbal responses such as "uh-huh . . . go on . . . really?" Use other acknowledgments such as nodding your head, smiling, leaning forward with interest, or sitting directly facing the speaker. Clarify points by asking questions or restating the points to be sure you are understanding the message the speaker is trying to convey.
- *Research.* Gather information about speaker, message, objectives, and the speaker's interests. Ask questions and gain feedback to get the speaker to open up and to feel more comfortable. Use empathy statements such as "it seems to me that you are frustrated because . . ." This can build a bond and can help the speaker restate or clarify statements.
- *Exercise Emotional Control.* Don't react emotionally to hot-button issues. Understand the message before you react to it. Recognize the symptoms of an emotional response (such as a facial flush, increased heartbeat) and redirect your thoughts so that you don't lose track of what the speaker is saying. Visualize calmness, pause, and try to find common ground. Try to understand what the speaker is saying before you react.
- *Sense the Nonverbal Message.* Try to understand nonverbal, body language, and visual messages. Some experts say that 90 percent of a message is carried by the vocal and visual channels, while only about 7 to 10 percent is carried by the verbal channels.
- *Structure.* Organize the information as you receive it to increase your retention. Take mental notes of the topic, the key points, and the reasoning behind the key points. Try to outline in your mind the speaker's speech. Listen for order or priority—for example, should something be done in a specific order? Is one thing more important than the other? Listen for consistency. Discriminate between pros and cons, fact and fiction.

Bob Schatz said, "One of the most highly respected sales people in my line of work is a guy who entered sales to overcome his innate shyness. He is very quiet and not the best public speaker in the world. He is a great listener, though, and there's no better friend a librarian can have in solving problems than this person. Watching this person succeed in sales reminds me that it isn't all about snappy patter or refined closing skills. It is about developing the respect of your customers. The route to building such respect can come from a variety of directions."

"Pay attention," urged Wayne Jones. "I try to adjust to their style if I can, but I also try to keep in mind the job or chore or task I am trying to get done. I think that is one of the lost arts in communication: paying attention."

ORGANIZATIONAL INTERACTION

One of the most difficult adjustments or learning curves for those new to the workplace is learning to work with various types of people. How do you learn to work in groups? How do you learn to work for a supervisor who doesn't think the same way you do?

When starting a new job (or when interviewing), watch the people around you. Notice how the supervisor makes decisions. Does he or she decide quickly or slowly? Does he take everyone's input into account, or does he make decisions based on one person's word? Does she move quickly or slowly? Does he like to communicate by e-mail or by conversation? Does she like being interrupted in her office or would she prefer you set an appointment?

Ask your coworkers to find out how things are done. Watch to see what works and what doesn't work. For example, does your supervisor get irritated when he or she is interrupted? Does she seem friendlier in the afternoon than the morning? Does he prefer large group interaction or one-to-one interaction? Does she prefer to have an e-mail or memo before a meeting, or does she like to think on her feet? Does he like to be out working with the employees or spend time in his office? All of these things can help you figure out how best to communicate with your new supervisor. Try to tailor your communication so that your message is heard and received in the best possible moment and format.

Do the same with your new coworkers. Do they get along? Do they criticize others, patrons, and the workplace? Do they look for the best in people? Are they enthusiastic and interested in their work? Do they go to each other to discuss problems, or do they go directly to the supervisor? Do they talk behind people's backs? Is there an atmosphere of trust?

Keep your eyes open for cliques. Don't get sucked into a group right away until you have gotten to know people better. You don't want to get labeled as part of a group until you've seen what everyone is like in the long run. Try not to become known as someone who's part of a clique. Be impartial and keep conversations as professional as possible.

Office politics take a long time to figure out; they are subtle and capricious. Play very carefully. Watch your coworkers. Be straightforward. Don't gossip.

Alison Hopkins explained, "I am part of a new administrative team in charge of the branches of my system. Previous administrations had had fairly poor relationships with support departments. Being friendly and listening to others has made a big difference, especially when it comes to information technology support. If you treat others with respect and try to understand their situation, then they do the same for you."

DIFFICULT SUPERVISORS

Try to understand what motivates your boss. Your boss won't be perfect. You may work for someone who's never managed anyone before. You may work for someone with an entirely different work style or personality than you have. Your boss's priorities are probably different than yours. You can't change your boss. Understanding what motivates your boss may help you develop some strategies for making the best of the situation. In her book *Rules for the Road: Surviving Your First Job Out of School*, Eve Luppert suggests motivations and techniques for working with several common types of supervisors.

- *Control Freak*. He is motivated by the fear that something will go wrong and he will be blamed. Try to anticipate his needs and provide it on time or early. One benefit of working for a control freak boss is that you'll learn every step of a process. As he sees that you anticipate needs, he will trust you and may become a great mentor for someone he trusts.
- *Hands-Off*. She is in the business to do her own thing, not to manage you. She doesn't have time to stop and explain to you, and won't be good at giving feedback. Find someone else who has done your job or does your job, and get guidance. Find the time when your boss is most receptive and have questions prepared then. Find a way to let your boss know what you're doing and what you've accomplished.

- *His Job Is Your Job.* Maybe this person is paid to strategize, but he doesn't get much done. Don't slack off because your boss seems to do so. Make sure you tell him how long an assignment will take when he assigns it. Doing your boss's work will give you a chance to learn things beyond your job and may prepare you for a job with more responsibility.
- *Let's Be Friends.* She wants to be liked or loved. She isn't good at drawing lines between her personal and professional life. Be friendly and persuasive, not confrontational. This boss can be a good mentor, often makes decisions by committee, and is often open about information.
- *Grouch.* He complains and criticizes all the time. Try to defend him to his detractors; this will build trust. Whenever you have a conflict at work, step back and develop a strategy. Don't react immediately. Don't take his criticism personally.

It is your responsibility to learn to get along with your boss. You can't change who he is, but you can control your behavior and expectations. Make sure you give your strategy time to work; be patient.

Camila Alire said, "If you are having trouble with a supervisor, ask yourself, is it you or is it the supervisor? Do others have trouble with this person? If the supervisor acts the same with everyone, then what can you do to work better with them? Find out from others what works and what doesn't. If you're the only one who has a problem with the supervisor, then do some self-reflection—is the problem affected by gender, race, personality? For example, does this person have trouble dealing with people of your gender? Are you contributing to the problem? If it's you, what can you do to change your behavior? If you are entry-level and the only one having trouble with a supervisor, the library director will not be too understanding. It's a challenge—a mark of a good supervisor is how they deal with personnel. Ask yourself, is this a functional institution? If not, then get out."

DIFFICULT COWORKERS

Not everyone will like you, and you won't like everyone. Focus on the work, not the people. Try to remain neutral with people you don't like. In her book, Eve Luppert shares some tips for dealing with some common types of difficult coworkers.

- *Plagiarist*. There are people who will take credit for your idea. You can interrupt the person in the meeting when they are presenting your idea, and try to say something like "when Joe and I were discussing this idea," and take control of the presentation. You might mention your idea to a couple folks before the meeting. Don't get too suspicious of everyone, though. Sometimes ideas are just common sense and more than one person has the same idea.
- *Gossip*. Be polite, look away as if you're busy, and change the subject. Don't tell this person anything you don't want broadcasted around the office. If you have to, be direct and tell this person you don't feel comfortable discussing the information they're sharing.
- *Harbinger of Doom*. Cynics drain you by complaining about everything but not suggesting a way to fix things. Try to get away from this person and think about your own experiences. Figure out what you can do about the bad things, to whom you can talk, and take action.
- *Talker*. Some people talk all day and prevent others from working. Smile, turn around, pick up the phone, and tell this person directly that you have a lot of work to do. This is a big step to learning to manage your time.
- *Fussbudget*. This is someone who has to have things done in a precise manner. Sometimes they have a good reason for wanting things done in a specific manner, so don't be irritated; maybe they are not explaining their reasoning well. Just do what they want, if possible. Try to learn to do things right the first time and meet deadlines.
- *Grudge Match*. Sometimes people may have it in for you. Maybe this person is threatened by you for some reason. Figure out what it is and attack that, not the person. Fight about work, not about people. Try to discover what threatens the person. Be polite and professional. Try not to begin hating the person back. Don't let the person know if you do hate them. A rule of thumb: If you hate one person, try to figure out what to do and move on. If you hate two people, tread carefully because the problem may be you. If you hate three people, it's definitely you, so take yourself off someplace and get over the problem.

Diversity in the workplace means that you work with people who do not think like you do. Don't assume everyone sees things the same way. Learn from people who are different. Leave your prejudices at the door.

Develop strategies for dealing with people you don't like or people who are difficult to be around. Try to stay away from them; but if you can't, develop stress reduction mechanisms. Stay professional. Try to return any criticism or complaining with positive comments or attitude, to diffuse (as much as you can) another person's negative attitude. If possible, talk with your supervisor, their supervisor, or a mentor about the problem. Perhaps you can be moved to a situation where you work with this person less.

"When I started at my first job I needed a particular person to do something for me," said Matt Wilcox. "This person was infamous for being difficult to work with, but because I had spent some time getting to know her I had no problems enlisting her help to get done what I needed done. Taking the time to chat a little with people, to see them as human beings, helps when you need something from them, and vice versa. It is easy to do things for your friends. If you don't have interpersonal skills, you had better be exceptionally good at what you do and be happy not working with the public. You have to really bring something to the table to make up for being a pain to work with. Interpersonal skills are everything. Of course, you have to get the work done and done well—one can only get by so long on charm."

ATTITUDE ADJUSTMENT

Examine yourself for bad habits. Look at yourself through others' eyes. What have you heard all your life from your parents, teachers, or friends? Is there merit in their criticisms? Will your new supervisor see these same habits? He or she will not be as lenient as people who love you.

Bad morale is catching. Make sure you don't take on others' miseries; focus on what has actually affected you personally. Fight your own battles. The workplace is not responsible for your happiness—you are. Bad morale is often caused by resistance to change, especially to change you can't control. When things change, you have to prove yourself over again. Change can be scary and difficult. View it as an opportunity to grow.

Beware of bad moods—if it is yours, try not to take it out on anyone else. If it is someone else's bad mood, don't take it personally. If someone else's bad mood persists one week, ask if there's anything you can do. Then let it go and move on.

SOCIAL SKILLS

Table manners count. At a meeting with food, focus on the agenda and not on the food. Don't let social skills get in the way of your message. At office parties or dinners, order what you want, but don't be excessive. Don't drink too much. Never drink more than the boss.

What if you hate parties? See what the corporate culture is. Are you expected to be at all functions? Are you only expected at one big event each year? These are sometimes things you can find out during an interview.

PERSONALITY TYPES

One method for getting along with almost anyone is recognizing that everyone thinks, acts, communicates, and reacts differently than you do. This sounds simplistic, but the ability to work with different types of people can be one of the most difficult skills to practice.

"I believe you must leave room for the differences," said Laura Sill. "You may need to adjust your style or strategy in approaching an issue to get the most out of the person you are working with. In other words, I try and focus on the other person—what they need to be successful. I think it's hard to change someone's style, so my plan is to work within their style when necessary. The result is that sometimes I feel frustration, but usually the outcome is good and the relationship remains strong."

Numerous books describe different methods for categorizing or describing people according to their personality type. A few popular typing mechanisms include the Myers-Briggs Type Indicator, the Marcus Paul, and the Enneagram. Whether you can recognize personality types or not, you will at least be more aware that people think and behave differently. Try to see things from others' points of view. Don't think you're always right. An organization will function most effectively when a variety of work styles are involved—imagine how little would get done, or how much would be missed, if the entire group were exactly alike!

Myers-Briggs Type Indicator (MBTI)

The Myers-Briggs Type Indicator is one of the most popular personality typing tools. This test divides people into sixteen personality types based on four basic dimensions: Extrovert vs. Introvert; Sensor vs. Intuitive; Thinker vs. Feeler; Perceptive vs. Judging. The words that Myers and Briggs used to describe these types are often misleading since the words have connotations in the normal language. Here are some basic characteristics of each dimension, according to Paul Tieger and Barbara Barron-Tieger's book, *The Art of Speedreading People.*

- *Extroverts* are other-centered. They get energy from being around other people and focus their energy on others. Extroverts crave external stimulation and are easily distracted. Extroverts get reenergized by being around others. They tend to jump into new social situations immediately. They are generalists who prefer to jump from topic to topic or from project to project. They think out loud. Extroverts are public people who tend to share more of themselves to the world. Extroverts make up about 50 percent of the American population.

- *Introverts* are self-centered, self-contained, self-reliant. They prefer to concentrate on projects that interest them. They are reenergized by being alone and are drained by too much activity or contact with others. They tend to watch an activity or social situation from the sidelines before becoming involved. Introverts are more likely to specialize or to focus on a topic in depth. They think through an idea before presenting it. They keep more to themselves and are more selective about sharing personal information with others. Introverts make up about 50 percent of the American population.

- *Sensors* pay more attention to what they are experiencing at the moment. Sensors think in a linear fashion. They prefer clear, tangible proof and are drawn to practical explanations. They trust experience and often find practical applications for something that has already been invented or established. They are drawn to familiar situations and ideas. Sensors enjoy setting up systems and following procedures so that things run smoothly. They often enjoy physical hobbies such as gardening. Sensors represent about 65 percent of the American population.

- *Intuitives* focus on the meaning or implications of something rather than the physical details. They tend to make intuitive jumps in their thinking instead of thinking in a linear fashion. They tend to be creative and can see possibilities or alternatives that may not be apparent to others. They do not need practical proof in order to believe something is possible. They are drawn to new and different ideas and are excited by change and possibilities. Intuitives are quickly bored with routine activity and are oriented toward the future. They are drawn to theoretical rather than the practical studies. They represent about 35 percent of the American population.

- *Thinkers* objectify a decision, weighing the pros, cons, and other practical ramifications. They analyze situations logically and objectively.

They are more satisfied in jobs that do not require them to pay attention to or respond to people's feelings. Thinkers value truth and honesty and will sometimes hurt people's feelings. They often appear cold and insensitive to Feelers. Feelers tend to be hurt more easily and Thinkers are often surprised that they were responsible for making this happen. They are convinced by a logical argument and are concerned with fairness. Thinkers make up about 50 percent of the American population, but about 65 percent of Thinkers are men.

- *Feelers* personalize a decision, focusing on personal values and the effect the decision will have on themselves and others. They are drawn to helping professions because of their innate need to help others. Feelers have a strong need to be liked and go to great lengths to please others. They value tact and diplomacy and will sometimes lie in order to save someone's feelings. They often appear soft and emotional to Thinkers. They are empathetic and sometimes do not make decisions based on logic, but on emotion. About 50 percent of the American population are Feelers, and about 65 percent of Feelers are women.

- *Judgers* like to decide or to have things settled. They feel tension until an issue is decided. They are more decisive so they tend to speak more authoritatively. They require less information to make a decision. They usually place a high importance on following rules. Because they are impatient with unsettled issues, they tend to step in and take charge. While Judgers may admire a Perceiver's ability to be spontaneous and to see all sides of an issue, they may also see a Perceiver as indecisive and procrastinating. Judgers are likely to be punctual and conscious of time and deadlines. They tend to be well organized. They are often compelled to finish their work before taking time off to play. Judgers make up about 60 percent of the American population.

- *Perceivers* like to leave things open. They feel tension when forced to make a decision. They are often slow to decide. They usually feel that rules are guidelines or are restrictions on their ability to be spontaneous. They are usually more able to see things in shades of gray. While Perceivers may admire a Judger's ability to make quick decisions, be organized, set goals, and get things done, they may also see a Judger as inflexible, uncompromising, and bossy. Perceivers are likely to be late and to procrastinate or to lose track of time. They are often disorganized. They are comfortable deferring work to relax or play. Perceivers represent about 40 percent of the American population.

The Myers-Briggs Type Indicator then categorizes people by combining the four dimensions—for example, an ESTJ would be someone with the Extrovert, Sensing, Thinking, and Judging characteristics. There are a number of similar type indicators on the Internet.

"One of the most useful tools we employed [at Vanderbilt University] was the Myers-Briggs tests," said Ann Ercelawn. "From this test I learned which colleagues prefer to communicate via phone and which via e-mail (and why). I try to remember these preferences in working with different individuals in my workplace."

Marcus Paul Placement Profile

"The Marcus Paul Placement Profile (MPPP) was developed using W. H. Marston's model of the four primary emotions and the research of J. P. Bauch and J. M. Nickens," explained Carol Ritzen Kem (sociology collection bibliographer, University of Florida), a consultant on the MPPP. "Nickens and Bauch's intention was to produce an instrument that would discern work behavior type for the purpose of matching individuals and jobs. The instrument is designed to be utilized as a tool in the educational setting for student personnel and placement as well as in the business setting for recruiting, job placement, work assignment, team building, and training (Bauch, 1981). Initially used for conducting research related to the theory of work behavior type, the MPPP is now available for use in workshops and seminars related to personality type and work behavior type."

The Marcus Paul Placement Profile categories people as four major types: Energizer, Inducer, Concentrator, and Producer. According to Kem's research, about 45 percent of academic librarians are Concentrators, 38 percent are Producers, 10 percent are Inducers, and only 7 percent are Energizers.

- *Energizers* are direct, assertive, creative, confident, highly motivated, highly productive, outspoken, decisive, competitive, and impatient with details. They expect immediate action, often become bored with the routine, and are most satisfied in a dynamic environment. They make quick decisions and naturally take charge in group situations.
- *Inducers* involve others as they pursue their objectives and are happiest when their work involves people. They are enthusiastic, inspiring, persuasive, sociable, and optimistic. They inspire teamwork and cooperation by using group processes to accomplish goals. They communicate skillfully and are often popular leaders.

- *Concentrators* are steady, attentive, committed, diplomatic, disciplined, orderly, patient, easygoing, and considerate. They apply their skills in an orderly manner and enjoy focusing on a task with minimum distractions. They are often very productive, accurate, and devoted to their profession.
- *Producers* strive for quality, follow procedures, and meet deadlines and standards. They appreciate stability, clear direction, and recognition for high performance in their work. They are accurate, agreeable, cautious, contented, exacting, logical, responsible, systematic, and loyal. They perform at their highest level if they are first given clear directions and understand exactly what is desired of them, so that they can fully commit to the task.

Enneagram

Another popular personality typing tool is the Enneagram, which divides people up into nine personality types. In his book *The Nine Ways of Working*, Michael Goldberg describes the nine types as they interact at work.

- *One*: The Perfectionist. They want to get things right and can be critical, idealistic, and judgmental. They have high standards for themselves and others. At their worst, their preaching and monitoring of others may make others feel rejected and intimidated, but their fiercest anger is directed at themselves. At their best, they are fastidious, upright, honest, idealistic, energetic, and have high powers of criticism and clear vision.
- *Two*: The Helper. They want to be appreciated for all they do for you. They are sweet, manipulative, and relationship-oriented. In order to gain power and influence, they make themselves indispensable to and appreciated by powerful people. They excel at customer service and have great intuition for the feelings, desires, and preferences of others. At their worst, Twos can be proud, manipulative, and ingratiating. At their best, Twos can be sensitive, helpful servants who lead by inspiring and bringing out the best in others.
- *Three*: The Producer. They want to be praised for getting the job done. They are enthusiastic, efficient, highly productive, competitive Type A's who want to be known for their many achievements. At their worst, Threes can be obsessed with image and approval, artificial, in-

sensitive, and superficial. At their best, Threes are charismatic leaders, motivators, efficient team leaders, and problem solvers.

- *Four*: The Connoisseur. They are artistic, melancholic, romantic, and elitist. They appreciate the beautiful, unusual, authentic, and "the best." They make decisions based on their deep feelings. At their worst, they can be intense, flamboyant, dramatic, snobby, elitist, and critical. At their best, they are creative, passionate, elegant people who live the good life with excellent taste.
- *Five*: The Sage. They are emotionally detached, intellectual, and want to be self-sufficient. They minimize needs and want to surround themselves with facts, theories, and information. At their worst, they are unfeeling, remote observers who hide behind data or expertise. At their best, they are brilliant, committed, respectful of boundaries, and can be excellent analysts, theorists, or advisers.
- *Six*: The Troubleshooter. They are preoccupied with what can go wrong. At their worst, they are paranoid and can overprepare, worry, and procrastinate. At their best, they are original and imaginative thinkers, faithful, sensitive, committed, courageous, and can be excellent at finding the hidden motives, concerns, and pitfalls of a project.
- *Seven*: The Visionary. They want to keep all options open, positive, and active. They are engaging, enthusiastic, energetic, innovative, upbeat planners. They have a hard time seeing the downside or pitfalls of a project and avoid closure, conflict, and routine work. They enthusiastically initiate projects but can fail to follow through. At their worst, they are narcissistic, irresponsible, and superficial. At their best, they are perceptive visionaries, charming idealists, inspirational, and enthusiastic networkers.
- *Eight*: The Top Dog. They want power and control. They are blunt, domineering, confrontational, and lack restraint. They feel and express feelings easily and loudly. At their worst, they are bullying, excessive, and unscrupulous. At their best, they are bold, entrepreneurial, protective leaders and empire builders.
- *Nine*: The Mediator. They want to include all people and ideas, and to avoid conflict. They are calming, compromise easily, and identify easily with others' needs, interests, and points of view. At their worst, Nines can be ambiguous, irrelevant, plodding bureaucrats. At their best, Nines are warm, openhearted, inspirational diplomats and team builders who help others reach decisions without their agenda intruding.

"When I went through an Enneagram workshop," said Bea Caraway (serials librarian, Trinity University), "I found out a coworker was a type Four and I was a One. I realized that the thing that irritated him the most was being corrected in public. I had been disagreeing with him by responding to group e-mail messages. Once I stopped doing that, our relationship became more congenial."

See table 5.1 for a few on-line personality typing resources. There are many other personality type tests. Whether you can identify someone's type or not, the important skill to develop is to understand that everyone is different and that what works for you may not work for those around you. Try to be sensitive and alert to the reactions of the people around you. Do they shy away or pull back when you barge into a room? Do they like to chatter all day when you would prefer to work quietly? How can you adapt your working and communication style so that you can work effectively with them?

"Understanding and appreciating personality and communications differences are the hardest things to overcome in the workplace," Bob Schatz agreed. "Identifying these differences and talking about how best to work

Table 5.1   On-line Personality Typing Resources

Personality Tests and Resources (St. Mary's University Academic
Library)
    http://library.stmarytx.edu/acadlib/subject/psych/prsnlty.htm

What Is the Myers-Briggs?
    http://gnd0.rmc.edu/administration/career_counseling/mbti.html

Humanmetrics Jung-Myers-Briggs Typology
    http://www.humanmetrics.com/cgi-win/JungType.htm

Enneagram Test
    http://graphics.lcs.mit.edu/~becca/enneagram/rheti/

Kaplan: Test Yourself
    http://www1.kaplan.com/view/article/0,1898,1411,00.html

Keirsey Temperament Sorter
    http://www.keirsey.com/cgi-bin/keirsey/newkts.cgi

Personality Tests on the WWW
    http://www.2h.com/Tests/personality.phtml

Test Junkie
    http://www.queendom.com/test_frm.html

Free Personality Tests by University of Life Inc-
    http://universityoflife.com/personalitytests.htm

around them is the best way to deal with them. For outgoing people, it is especially hard to appreciate the value of those who are quieter and more easily intimidated. A real effort has to be made to accommodate their needs for more time and space into which to respond. Conversely, quiet people need to appreciate the value of those who can bring some energy and excitement to their work. In either case, developing good listening skills will be essential. This can be a very demanding task for those who are not by nature good listeners."

SUMMARY

- Learn to communicate with different types of people. Learn to listen effectively.
- Be aware of your organizational culture. Try to communicate and interact effectively to be productive.
- Learn to work effectively with difficult supervisors or coworkers.
- Adjust your own attitude when necessary.
- Learn to act appropriately in social situations.
- Recognize that people with different personality types will think, act, and respond differently. Try to adapt your communication and work style to be as productive as possible when working with various personality types.

RELATED READING

Interpersonal Skills

Bell, Arthur H., and Dayle M. Smith. *Winning with Difficult People*. Hauppauge, N.Y.: Barron's Educational Series, 1997.

Dolphin, Philippa. "Interpersonal Skills Training for Library Staff." *Library Association Record* 88 (March 1986): 134.

Feldman, David. "Leadership As a Resource—Interpersonal Skills." *Aslib Proceedings* 39 (October 1987): 299–301.

Levy, Philippa. "Interpersonal Skills and Trainer Development: Using the Six Category Model." *Personnel Training and Education* 7, no. 1 (1990): 3–8.

Levy, Philippa, and Robert C. Usherwood. "Putting People First (Interpersonal Skills Training)." *Library Association Record* 91 (September 1989): 526.

Odini, Cephas. "Training in Interpersonal Skills for Librarians and Information Workers." *Library Review (Glasgow, Scotland)* 40, no. 4 (1991): 6–20.

Communication

Alessandra, Tony, and Phil Hunsaker. *Communicating at Work: Improve Your Speaking, Listening, Presentation, and Correspondence Skills to Get More Done and Get What You Want at Work.* New York: Fireside, 1993.
Association of Research Libraries. "Interpersonal Communication Skills." In *Developing Leadership Skills: A Sourcebook for Librarians,* edited by Rosie L. Albritton. Englewood, Colo.: Libraries Unlimited, 1990.
Chapman, Linda. "Building Effective Communication Skills: Reading, Writing, and Speaking Resources." *Information Searcher* 12, no. 1 (2000): 8–17.
Howlett, Barbara. "Communication Skills and Strategies for Teacher-Librarians." In *The School Library Program in the Curriculum,* edited by Ken Haycock. Englewood, Colo.: Libraries Unlimited, 1990.
Kratz, Abby Robinson. "Communication Skills." In *Practical Help for New Supervisors,* edited by Joan Giesecke. Chicago, Ill.: American Library Association, 1997.
Kratz, Dennis, and Abby Robinson Kratz. *Effective Listening Skills.* Chicago, Ill.: Irwin Professional Publishers, 1995.
Luppert, Eve. *Rules for the Road: Surviving Your First Job Out of School.* New York: The Berkley Publishing Group, 1998.
Nichol, James W. "Zen and the Art of User Friendly Service: 2—Communication Skills." *State Librarian* 36 (July 1988): 19–21.
Yang, Eveline L. "Personal Communication Skills Essential for Public Relations." *Colorado Libraries* 13 (September 1987): 8–10.

Attitude Adjustment

Intner, Sheila S. "Stream of Consciousness: the Importance of Attitude." *Technicalities* 18, no. 1 (January 1998): 2–3.
Malia, Elizabeth. "Professional Is an Attitude." *Library Mosaics* 8 (January/February 1997): 12–13.

Personality Types

Alessandra, Tony, and Michael J. O'Conner. *The Platinum Rule: Discover the Four Basic Business Personalities—And How They Can Lead You to Success.* New York: Warner Books, 1996.
Goldberg, Michael J. *Getting Your Boss's Number.* San Francisco: Harper Collins, 1996.

————. *The Nine Ways of Working: How to Use the Enneagram to Discover Your Natural Strengths and Work More Effectively*. New York: Marlowe, 1999.

Kem, Carol Ritzen. "The Relationship between Work Behavior Type and Elements of Job Satisfaction of a Selected Group of Academic Librarians," *Advances in Library Administration and Organization* 17 (2000): 23–66.

Kroeger, O., and J. M. Theusen. *Type Talk at Work*. New York: Delacorte Press, 1992.

Scherdin, M. J. *Discovering Librarians: Profiles of a Profession*. Chicago: American Library Association, 1994.

Tieger, Paul D., and Barbara Barron-Tieger. *The Art of Speedreading People: How to Size People Up and Speak Their Language*. Boston: Little, Brown, 1998.

CHAPTER 6

Mentoring

Except for socially, you're my role model.

—Blair Litton, *Broadcast News* (1987)

A good mentor can help you navigate library school, your job search, your first job, and your career. Mentors can also introduce you to others, can broaden your network, and can share their knowledge. By keeping a mentor up to date on what you're doing, he or she can sometimes suggest career paths or solutions to problems.

"I was selected to participate in a wonderful year-long program called SunSeekers that was sponsored by SEFLIN (the consortium of public and academic libraries in southeast Florida)," described Teresa Abaid (technical services librarian, Florida Atlantic University). "The program was initiated because of a concern locally that there were not enough leaders entering the profession to replace those who were retiring. I was in the second class of SunSeekers. We each selected a mentor at our first meeting after being introduced to those (a variety of administrators on different levels) who had volunteered to become mentors. I chose a lady who is the associate director from Florida International University. The match was most successful and I had the best year in my professional life. The program had monthly daylong workshops at which we were exposed to various speakers, personality diagnostic tests, etc. These workshops combined with the monthly luncheon meetings that I had with my mentor were very profitable. At the meetings with my mentor, I discussed concerns I had with committees or handling a problem at work. Although I was not a new librarian, I was returning to the field after a seventeen-year hiatus and I found the program and the mentor/mentee relationship very beneficial."

Susan Davis remembered how a mentor helped her. "A mentor recommended me to write an important article, and then recommended me to do it again the next year," said Davis. "She had also helped me become involved in a state organization by suggesting I volunteer to be a committee chair."

SEEK OUT MENTORS

You can meet mentors anywhere—at work, in your community, professional associations, social groups, churches, or elsewhere. Look for people whom you admire and people you would like to model yourself after. Don't be afraid to ask them questions. Sometimes mentors just "happen" informally—you'll find that you become friends with someone whom you consider a role model. Tap into their expertise and experience; keep them up on what you're doing; ask their advice about job searches, difficulties at work, or anything.

"Attend conferences and meetings, especially local or regional ones, to make some contacts," Susan Davis encouraged. "Look for opportunities where you could make a contribution, even if only a small one. Meet and talk with others with similar interests, perhaps a speaker at a session you particularly enjoyed."

Bob Schatz said, "If you respect someone else and they have knowledge that would be of use or interest to you, just ask them if they would mind explaining that thing, or if they would mind if you watched them work. If mentoring is meant to be, it will naturally grow into a relationship where teaching and learning take place. In a real, natural mentoring relationship, both people teach and both people learn, and that's a natural by-product of personal regard and mutual respect."

Sometimes you can find mentors in a more formal manner. For example, the American Library Association New Members Round Table sponsors a conference mentoring program that matches a new conference attendee with a mentor at the ALA conference. Several other professional organizations offer this sort of program. Sometimes formal pairings such as these can lead to a continued relationship.

Michelle Mach (Web librarian, Colorado State University Libraries) said, "Many libraries have formal mentoring programs, but don't limit yourself to them. In academic libraries with tenure systems, mentors in formal programs are usually tenured faculty. However, often the wisest and most honest advice I received was from nontenured librarians who were two or three years ahead of me on the tenure track. Because they were going through the process themselves, their advice tended to be direct and to the point. Mentoring is especially helpful for making those personal connections in your organization or in the field. It is so much easier to send off that e-mail or pick up the phone and say that 'so and so' suggested that I talk to you about 'project x' rather than making that cold contact."

"Ask someone to be your mentor," urged Jim Walther. "Use those words—'Will you be my mentor?' It's flattering—it shows them you admire them and you admit you need to learn something you don't know."

Be careful that you are not asking too much of someone who already is very busy, and is perhaps mentoring several other people. It's often best to develop these relationships in a more informal way. Maybe you can meet these people through people you already know. Maybe you can become involved in a committee that they're involved in. Maybe you can volunteer to help them with a project or program.

Kathie Henderson (professor, University of Illinois Graduate School of Library and Information Science) wrote, "The mentors that we have used in our classes have, in some respects, become the professional mentors for our students in some cases. Look around you in your job or at professional meetings. Read discussion lists and find those you admire. A good mentor is not too different from a good leader. Listening and observing are perhaps the best qualifications for a good mentor. It is important that the mentee is completely honest with the mentor, that the mentee has some good questions to ask and doesn't always depend on the mentor to make the overtures. It is hard to help if you don't know what is needed.

"I still remember how a mentor helped me on my first day as a serials cataloger after library school," continued Henderson. "I knew how to catalog, but not exactly the protocol to start the process in the job. The serials cataloger sitting next to me sensed that and gave me some copies of her copy slips (this was precomputer days) to look at. I will never forget her kindness in helping me get started in that situation. Naturally, I turned to her on many occasions after that."

WHAT MAKES A GOOD MENTOR?

"I'm not sure that there is any special formula for a good mentor," suggested Susan Davis. "Since it's a relationship, you have to find a good fit with mentor and mentee. What are the mentee's goals? In general, I'd say that you need to find someone with similar interests, who can give you good advice, and can help you find opportunities to contribute to the profession."

Laura Sill said, "In a mentor, I look for an individual who wants to take a genuine interest in who I am as a professional. I look for someone who is familiar with my work or area of librarianship. I look for someone who is a good listener, but someone who also gives advice and encouragement to me.

In a mentee, I look for an individual who is interested in dialog; someone who is willing to share his experiences."

"In a mentor I look for someone who listens patiently, who takes the time to explain thoroughly, and who has confidence in my abilities," said Ann Ercelawn.

"A mentor can be anyone whom you like or trust," Ann Green (librarian, Sonnenschein Nath & Rosenthal) added. "I would look for someone whose career path you want to emulate."

Richard Murray said, "I think people looking for mentors—whether they're working as student assistants, paraprofessionals, or in their first professional position—often gravitate towards their supervisor because it's convenient. Having their supervisor serve in a mentoring role works for some people; these people are doubly lucky to have a great boss who's willing and able to be a mentor. But I'd advise people to be cautious. The boss/employee relationship is a tricky one, even under the best of circumstances. Even if you've got the best boss in the world, eventually you'll have a disagreement over something, and if you've had a true mentoring relationship with that person, negotiating your way to a solution can be trickier.

"It might be preferable—and safer—to look to others in your department or, maybe even better, in another department within your library (assuming you're looking within your own organization, which certainly isn't a requirement). In a previous job, I found a mentor figure who worked in a completely different department within the library, and this really helped me out. When I went to her to vent about problems I was having, she could look at them from an outsider's perspective, something I wouldn't have gotten from a boss who was also a mentor. We established a really supportive relationship, and even though I don't even work at that university anymore, I still go to her when I need advice, self-validation, or a kick in the rear end (delivered lovingly, of course).

"Again," continued Murray, "I don't want to say that a boss cannot also be a mentor. I've seen people develop wonderful, supportive mentoring relationships with their supervisors. But I've also seen people go down in flames, so be careful.

"Look for someone supportive and comforting and willing to provide a shoulder to cry on, but also someone with a spine and someone who will tell you when you're being ridiculous. Occasionally, almost all of us want to engage in a good old-fashioned game of 'Poor Me,' and it's much more fun with a receptive audience. You need somebody who's willing to listen, hand out tissues, pat you on the head, and say 'There, there!' But an excellent mentor will give you a good dose of tea and sympathy and then point you in the right direction. Or tell you when you're being silly and to stop feeling sorry for yourself. You need someone who's grounded in reality and who'll give you what's best for you, whether it seems that way at the time or not. It's all well and good to have somebody who'll do the tear-in-your-beer routine with you, but to get something positive out of the experience there has to be something more constructive at the end."

BE A PROACTIVE PROTÉGÉ

Don't wait for others to teach you things. Ask questions. Ask supervisors, coworkers, employees, mentors, colleagues, friends, vendors, and others in your professional or personal circles—most people will be glad to help you or teach you something new. Your supervisors will often not have a formal training program and will rely on you to tell them what you need to know.

"Mentees need to feel comfortable asking for the mentor's time," said Angela Horne (public services librarian, Johnson Graduate School of Management Library). "Too often, the mentoring pairs fail to establish guidelines at the beginning of their pairing (frequency of meetings, expectations of each other, personal goals, length of the pairing, etc.), and this leads to misunderstanding and the potential for hurt. Some mentees never realize they needn't wait for their mentor to call a meeting.

"My first job out of library school was a two-month summer position, and at the end of the summer my boss asked me to stay on and take responsibility for a project I thought I was unqualified to undertake. She had no doubts that I'd be more than able to handle my new tasks, and I ended up both loving the position and winning a major library award for my work. She always believed in my core abilities and never failed to boost my spirits when I was feeling frustrated. After I left that organization she became a true friend, someone I still consider a mentor but also much more than that label can ever signify."

Ann Green agreed. "I was a paralegal in a large D.C. law firm when the librarians at that law firm befriended me. They said 'Why be a paralegal? With your research skills, you should go to library school,' so I did. I have never regretted that decision. I think the biggest mistake new professionals make is waiting for someone 'right' to mentor them and waiting for someone to help them. Don't wait—go out and listen to older and more experienced librarians. Make your own connections and go from there! You only get somewhere if you do it yourself."

Be proactive in finding out what you don't know. Attend conferences, read, continue learning, talk with colleagues, etc. Focus on a new area for a month or so to develop new skills. Ask your mentors what skills they find invaluable in an employee.

Marcia Keyser (librarian, Texas A&M University Kingsville) said, "I was surprised to find, after I'd been in library school for several months, that a close family friend was a librarian. Even though she's in a different sort of library, she has lots of experience and technical knowledge that has been helpful, and she was active in a professional organization. Also, retain contacts in your early nonprofessional library positions, or practicums, if you do any of these. Finding somebody who has ever done what you are trying to do is always helpful. Whatever project you need to undertake in your library, or to write and publish about, etc., someone else has probably done something similar. And don't dismiss other types of librarians. School, public, academic, or special—we all can share quite a bit. You may not be able to find the perfect mentor who has the exact position that you aspire to."

Let your mentors know when you are looking for a new job. They can often guide you, tell you about a particular workplace, put you in contact with influential people, serve as references, etc.

Laura Sill commented, "My mentor has provided me with opportunities through ALA. She has also watched my behavior and work, and advised me on how to improve myself professionally (this has included telling me when I didn't act or perform as well as I could have)."

Associate with positive people, people who inspire you to do your best. Surround yourself with positive people—people who are generally upbeat and have a positive, proactive attitude toward their work, life, and career. If you're around negative people, you will develop a negative or fatalistic attitude. Surround yourself with people who are in control of their lives and careers. You will learn good habits from them, and they will inspire and encourage you when you're down. Associate with people who work hard and will push you to do your best. Even a competitive relationship can help you work harder, as long as the relationship isn't a jealous one.

"Mentoring should be a natural offshoot of a good personality fit with mutual personal and professional respect," said Bob Schatz. "When those elements exist, I think mentoring happens naturally. Of course, a good mentor has to desire to help someone else on the way up. And a good mentee has to want to learn what someone with more experience can offer. If those things aren't there, the mentoring process will be artificial and will likely fail. As with other things in professional work, you can teach skills, but you can't teach a person to be genuine and caring. Those who have those qualities will grow and help others to grow. Those who don't, probably won't.

"First of all," Schatz continued, "let me say that most mentoring takes place without either mentor or mentee thinking of it as a mentoring process. You only discover that when you look back on the experience. A mentor I had in my early work life was a great friend and someone who was well loved by booksellers and librarians both. Through his friendship, patience, and advice, he taught me not to become too full of myself, and to have a forgiving enough heart to give people who had erred another chance to show their true colors. If they were worthy of forgiveness, it was worth extending it to them."

PITFALLS OF POPULARITY: AN ESSAY

by Jill Emery
Director, Electronic Resources Program, University of Houston

As with every profession, library and information sciences have celebrities and stellar institutions. Sometimes, these are regional LIS gurus or nationally recognized personalities due to their astute knowledge of some facet of LIS, their tremendous publishing capabilities, and/or the roles they may play in regional and national professional organizations. Sometimes, these are institutions or companies known for their advancement of the profession or their professionals. In either case, both scenarios make for an attractive working environment and hold the potential of a premier mentoring experience. However, it is better to walk into a situation forearmed as opposed to having your eyes wide shut.

1. *Destroy Your Idols*: There are many Jekyll and Hyde types within our profession. Who a person is at conference, giving a lecture, or appearing in print may bear little resemblance to who they are within a company or institutional setting. Get to know the staff at the organization prior to applying. If you're looking for that mentoring atmosphere, ask questions about the celebrity to find out the role the person plays in the organization, how he interacts with all levels of staff, and how mentoring or nurturing he is capable of being to you.
2. *Escape from Alcatraz*: Learn about the organization in which this person works. Perhaps they are so professionally involved because it is a strict tenure environment that requires rabid professional participation. Or perhaps these people are miserable in their jobs but are able to maintain

a day-to-day existence because they can escape into their professional responsibilities. You don't want to end up in an unsupportive, drab environment where your only recourse for happiness is being a consummate professional. Look for a congenially, supportive environment. The more the staff act like family, the better the place is to allow such freedom and growth as an individual within a team setting.

3. *Avoid Poison Ivy*: Trying to get a job at an institution or company because it is one of "the companies" or "the institutions" is not always wise. There are many wonderful, elite places to work but make sure you'll fit in there, and that you're not applying for the name alone. For one, those interviewing you will pick up on your status infatuation and it may cost you the job.

4. *Caveat Mentor*: Say you meet this great person at a conference or at a professional activity and they mention a job opening under them or in their department. If you want to stay with this person for a while in a professional relationship, make sure they are invested in the place at which they work. There's nothing worse than moving 3,000 miles to work with someone who changes jobs in a year's time. This happens more often than you may think it does. One way to avoid this trap is to partner with someone you respect and admire on a project that you will present at a professional conference or meeting.

5. *Celebrity Skin*: If your goal is to work for or to be mentored by one of LIS's big kahunas, make sure you really know them and their quirks. Don't become a corporate coffee drone, a whipping child, or a servant. If you have to have a close professional relationship, learn what roles you can play to be supportive to them. Learn to be indispensable, creative, and proactive. Try to absorb their better attributes but never, ever, mimic anyone.

MENTOR OTHERS

Even as a new librarian or someone very new in the field, you can still mentor others. In fact, newer professionals tend to be more aware of concerns that students or other new information professionals may have. Maybe there is someone thinking about going into librarianship. Maybe it's the classified staff members you work with, who don't want to earn an MLS but who do want to do a good job. Maybe it's volunteers or student workers. Maybe it's children in the community. Take time to mentor others, either as you have been mentored or as you wish you had!

Connie Foster (serials librarian, Western Kentucky University) described one of her mentoring experiences. "I began thinking about the importance of promoting librarianship as a career when Anne Beaubien spoke at the joint Kentucky Library Association/Tennessee Library Association academic sections in April 1991, when the ACRL theme for the year was recruitment. Most of the issues and literature at that time focused on library school students. To my way of thinking, we had to capture students at a much younger age in order to inspire and inform them about the joys of academic librarianship, as well as other types of librarianship.

"I noticed that our community had a strong 4-H Career Shadowing program, and I got on their mailing list (forever). In October 1993, I sent a memo to my department head about my desire to promote librarianship as a career. On March 2, 9, and 16, 1993 (usually there are three days for this and we choose at least one—sometimes one date inevitably falls during our spring break), we began career shadowing in technical services. Although the program is for fifth through twelfth grades, we usually had a fifth- or sixth-grade student. To make the day pass really quickly, at least two of us shadow and one is the primary host. We tour all areas of the library and then share with cataloging, acquisitions, and serials for forty-five minutes of hands-on work. I have been doing this for most years since 1993 and find it extremely rewarding. We have an agenda, a fact sheet, and put together a folder of stuff about the library (and of course, bookmarks). We eat lunch together and the day does really fly by because they leave around 3:00 and arrive at 9:00 a.m.

"We also did a mini-session at a Kentucky Library Association meeting shortly after (title: In Touch with the Future: Promoting Librarianship as a Career) and showed photos of our shadowers, information created, etc. Although some are very scared at first, by the end of the day you have to "fight" for your desk again. Most are computer literate and e-mail adept; all are eager and have had to prepare a booklet and do research ahead of time and then report afterwards.

"Although we don't really know the long-term effects of this experience," Foster concluded, "I am sure it at least plants a seed and lets students see libraries as fun places to work and hopefully more than just gatekeepers of collections. We stress the skills needed, degrees, professional development, etc. I'm sure lots of that goes way over their heads but who knows what impact this will have on their futures. If not librarianship, then perhaps anything that requires a good education."

Jay Bhatt (engineering information services librarian, Drexel University) offered, "We, at Hagerty Library-Drexel University, developed a program for our library assistants and information science and technology students, who are graduate students in Drexel's College of Information Science and Technology program. This program started with our dean's vision of training, mentoring, and acquiring professional training and skills while in the program. As part of this program, each student can have a member from our professional staff as a mentor. Each month, the professional staff member takes the student to the faculty club where the student has an opportunity to talk about various issues pertaining to library and career. Students also have an opportunity to take minutes in various professional staff meetings."

Mentoring others is not only your responsibility—it also helps you learn. As someone else asks your opinion, you often have to find the answer or reexamine your viewpoints. It also helps you remember what it's like to be a student, for example. It helps you see what others are going through. It helps you broaden your experience by seeing others' experiences. It can prompt you to see issues from a different perspective. As you progress through your career, continue to learn from and mentor others in order to keep growing and giving.

SUMMARY

- Seek out mentors throughout your career.
- Be proactive in interacting with your mentor. Don't be afraid to make contact and keep them informed of your activities, questions, and problems.
- Surround yourself with positive and proactive people.
- Mentor others. Look for ways you can help students or other new information professionals.

RELATED READINGS

Mentoring

Abif, Khafre K. "A Commitment to Mentoring." *American Libraries* 30, no. 3 (March 1999): 60.

Colley, Joanne, and Connie Capers Thorson. "Mentoring along the Tenure Track (Helping New Library Faculty Members Meet Their Goals)." *College & Research Libraries News,* no. 4 (April 1990): 297–300.

DeShane, Abby. "Mentoring: An Annotated Bibliography." *Business and Finance Division Bulletin,* no. 113 (winter 2000): 23–9.

Farmer, Jane C. "Identifying the Transferable Skills of Information Professionals through Mentoring." *Education for Information* 16, no. 2 (June 1998): 95–106.

Fisher, Biddy. "Do As I Do (Mentoring As Part of Continuing Professional Development)." *Library Association Record* 99, no. 10 (October 1997): 544–5.

Fisher, Biddy. *Mentoring*. London: Library Association, 1994.

Ginanni, Katy. "Preparing Tomorrow's Serial Leaders: Creating New Alliances among Library Schools, Libraries, and Serial Professionals." *The Serials Librarian* 28, no. 3–4 (1996): 291–5.

Golian, Linda Marie. "Effective Mentoring Programs for Professional Library Development." *Advances in Library Administration and Organization* 14 (1996).

Johnson, Margaret Ann. "Mentoring." *Technicalities* 17, no. 8 (September 1997): 1.

Jones-Quartey, Theo S. "Mentoring—Personal Reflections of a Special Librarian." *Information Outlook* 4, no. 7 (July 2000): 26–30.

Kirkland, Janice. "The Missing Women Library Directors: Deprivation versus Mentoring." *College & Research Libraries* 58 (July 1997): 376–84.

Lary, Marilyn Searson. "Mentoring: A Gift for Professional Growth." *The Southeastern Librarian* 47, no. 4 (1998): 23–6.

Lee, Janet. "Mentoring in Our Midst." *Colorado Libraries* 19 (spring 1993): 54.

Lewandowski, Fabian. "Trustees Mentoring Trustees." *Public Libraries* 37, no. 3 (May/June 1998): 172–4.

Maack, Mary Niles. *Aspirations and Mentoring in an Academic Environment: Women Faculty in Library and Information Science*. Westport, Conn.: Greenwood Press, 1994.

"Mentoring: A Key Resource to Develop Professional and Personal Competencies." *Information Outlook* 3, no. 2 (February 1999): 12.

Moen, William E. "Mentoring: Protection and Permission (to Be Yourself)." *Library Personnel News* 3 (fall 1989): 50.

Munde, Gail. "Beyond Mentoring: Toward the Rejuvenation of Academic Libraries." *The Journal of Academic Librarianship* 26, no. 3 (May 2000): 171–5.

Nankivell, Clare. "Mentoring in Library and Information Services: A Literature Review and Report on Recent Research." *New Review of Academic Librarianship* 3 (1997): 91–144.

Riley, Cheryl. "Academic Librarians and Mentoring Teams: Building Tomorrow's Doctorates." *Technical Services Quarterly* 14, no. 3 (1997): 1–10.

Roberts, Deanna L. "Mentoring in the Academic Library." *College & Research Libraries News*, no. 2 (February 1986): 117–19.

Rouse, Mary Ellen. "Mentoring." *New Jersey Libraries* 26, no. 2 (1993): 13–5.

Stalcup, Sue S. "Mentoring: A Tool for Career Enhancement." *Library Personnel News* 3 (winter 1989): 4–5.

Taylor, Valerie S. "Mentoring: A Key Resource to Develop Professional and Personal Competencies." *Information Outlook* 3, no. 2 (February 1999): 12.

Tolson, Stephanie D. "Mentoring up the Career Ladder." *Information Outlook* 2, no. 6 (June 1998): 37–8.

Trickey, Keith V. "A Different Kind of Training and Education." *Library Associa-tion Record* 99, no. 10 (October 1997): 546.
Van Deusen, Jean Donham, and Anne Marie Kraus. "Mentoring: A Professional Growth Strategy for School Library Media Specialists." *School Library Media Activities Monthly* 11 (March 1995): 29–31.

Electronic Mentoring

Echavarria, Tami. "Encouraging Research through Electronic Mentoring: A Case Study." *College & Research Libraries* 56 (July 1995): 352–61.
Henderson, Kathryn Luther. "Electronic Keyboard Pals: Mentoring the Electronic Way." *The Serials Librarian* 29, no. 3–4 (1996): 141–64.
Kindon, Victoria. "Match Game: Learning from the E-Mentoring Program to Most Effectively Match Mentors and Protégés." Thesis, University of North Carolina at Chapel Hill, 2000.

Formal Mentoring Programs

Boylston, Susanna D. "ACRL's New Member Mentoring Program: Make a Com-mitment to Professional Development." *College & Research Libraries News* 61, no. 3 (March 2000): 204–5.
Dragovich, Pamela. "Alma Mater Mentoring: Library Science Alumni Promote School and Profession." *Journal of Education for Library and Information Sci-ence* 36 (fall 1995): 346–50.
Farmer, Jane C. "Identifying the Transferable Skills of Information Professionals through Mentoring." *Education for Information* 16, no. 2 (June 1998): 95–106.
Jesudason, Melba. "Mentoring New Colleagues: A Practical Model from the Uni-versity of Wisconsin-Madison." *Illinois Libraries* 79 (winter 1997): 23–30.
Kochoff, Stephen T. "The Division's Mentoring Initiative: Sharing Knowledge to Advance Your Career." *Business and Finance Division Bulletin,* no. 111 (spring 1999): 9–10.
Parris, Carol J. "A Library Mentoring Program for the Millennium." *Kentucky Li-braries* 64, no. 2 (spring 2000): 11–14.
Ritchie, Ann. "Professionalism through ALIA: Outcomes from Group Mentoring Programs." *Australian Library Journal* 48, no. 2 (May 1999): 160–77.
Wittkopf, Barbara J. "Mentoring in Academic Libraries: LSU Libraries Model." *LLA Bulletin* 61, no. 4 (spring 1999): 226–32.
———. "Mentoring Programs in ARL Libraries." Thesis, University of North Car-olina at Chapel Hill, 1999.
Wojewodzki, Catherine. "Formalizing an Informal Process: Developing a Mentor-ing Program in a University Library." *Technical Services Quarterly* 15, no. 3 (1998): 1–19.

CHAPTER 7

Leadership Skills

First rule of leadership: everything is your fault.

—Hopper, *A Bug's Life* (1998)

What makes a good leader? In their book *Learning to Lead*, Warren Bennis and Joan Goldsmith list four personal qualities that people want to see in their leader. These qualities are vision, trust, optimism, and action.

1. *Purpose, Direction, Meaning*: Leaders should have direction and purpose, but also must be able to communicate it clearly to others so that they own the vision as well.
2. *Trust*: Trust is built on openness. "We cannot overemphasize the importance of encouraging openness, even dissent," state Bennis and Goldsmith.
3. *Optimism*: Leaders must have a clear vision of the future and the commitment to get there. They must also be able to encourage and inspire others to come along.
4. *Action and Results*: It's not enough to have great ideas. A good leader must convert ideas into action.

LEADERS VS. MANAGERS

There are differences between a leader and a manager. A leader is innovative and adaptive, while a manager copies previous actions or maintains the status quo. A leader is effective where a manager is efficient. A leader inspires, empowers, and engages others in her vision of the future. A leader pulls rather than pushes.

"A leader stands up for what is right and conducts him/herself in a way that others will naturally be willing to follow," said Bob Schatz. "This usually comes from showing that you have a commitment to the people who answer to you, as well as requiring a commitment from them. Managers oversee processes, but rarely inspire people to do more than meet the officially stated demands of the task."

Jim Walther added, "A manager controls resources or people. A leader is an earned title, opposite of manager. Why do people lead? It's things they decided to do. They have earned trust."

"Note the excellent examples of the true leaders around them," urged Angela Horne. "If you have a superb supervisor, or know of someone else in your organization who is well respected and exudes leader qualities, analyze why those individuals are so adept at what they do. Deconstruct their habits and personal style. Observe them in meetings, and in social situations, and wherever else you come into contact with them. Which of their qualities are ones you yourself could begin to emulate? Also, having a supervisory position most definitely isn't an end all and be all of leadership. All too often people are promoted to supervisory roles before they are ready to assume care of another's career. Take managerial classes. Attend lectures in your organization or community on the topic of supervision. Read the literature. Who are the figures in the modern world who you feel are the best leaders? Why?"

Laura Sill said, "Skills that are essential for a leader include listening, the ability to motivate, the ability to articulate and sell a vision, the ability to strategize any given situation, the ability to see the big picture. To me, management is an activity and leadership is a way of thinking and acting."

"A leader has a vision of what s/he is trying to accomplish and is proactive," Ann Ercelawn added. "Also a leader is not afraid to tackle problems head-on. Managers are continually coping with problems that they didn't anticipate, or chose to ignore hoping that they would go away—rarely the case!"

QUALITIES OF LEADERSHIP

Integrity

Being in a leadership position can be a power trip. Don't let it go to your head. A good leader must take a stand for what he believes in and make that vision a reality, yet he must control his ambition and ego. A good leader balances ambition, competence, and integrity. You must look out for others rather than yourself.

A good leader has integrity, keeps promises, is trustworthy, and is not egotistical or insecure. He does not try to control through fear. A good leader is not afraid to admit he/she doesn't know something and is not threatened by others who have more experience. He is constantly learning.

"Failures are better learning experiences," said Jim Walther. "Honest integrity will earn trust. With management, it's the structure that leads; leadership, it's your vision that leads you. Identify what you're doing in broad view, not a limited view of job titles."

Trust

Above all, a leader must create an atmosphere of trust. Trust is created when employees feel free to express dissent. To create trust, a leader must show that he is competent. Employees will lose faith in an employer who does not show competence. A leader must have congruity or integrity. In other words, what the leader does must be congruous with what he says or feels or states as his vision. A leader must be supportive. Followers must feel that their leader is on their side, and that she will defend them if necessary. A leader must care about others and about the impact his actions or decisions will have on the group.

Trust your employees, coworkers, teammates. Try to inspire trust in them. A good leader inspires the trust of others and trusts them to do a good job. Empower others and give them authority to make decisions.

"A good leader," said Angela Horne, "should have compassion, the ability to listen, intelligence, humility, vision, the ability to speak at all levels (explaining ideas to people at all levels of the organization), accountability, integrity, self-confidence, and continuous respect for one's colleagues and subordinates."

Charisma

Be enthusiastic. Charisma and enthusiasm can win a lot of supporters. Help people see the purpose or goal of the project or the institution. Try to make work enjoyable and have a genuine interest in improving service or production or whatever your goal is.

"I have always told my students that they can learn from any situation," Kathie Henderson advised. "There are good supervisors and then there are bad ones. What one learns from the bad ones is what not to do when one is the supervisor or leader. What one learns from the good ones is what worked for them in a particular situation. This may not work for another person in another situation, but it is a good starting point. Leadership skills are not something one reads in a book or can be taught in library school although students always think that they can come from some lessons learned in school. They are very much an individual response to an individual situation although there are common threads to many situations. But a good leader must analyze carefully each situation.

"A leader is enthusiastic, responsive to needs, knows the situation and those who work with him/her. A leader knows when to lead and when to let go. A leader encourages and praises good results. A leader also has to let those with whom he/she works know when expectations are not being met. A leader listens and observes carefully and does not make snap judgments."

DEVELOPING LEADERSHIP SKILLS

In your first job, you're often not in a traditional leadership role. You will still have opportunities to lead, and to develop your leadership skills. Look for opportunities such as committees, special projects, teams, professional involvement, community involvement, etc. Chair a committee in a professional organization, volunteer to coordinate a special project at work, and so on.

Ann Green encouraged, "Volunteer with a professional association such as Law Librarians Society of D.C. or your equivalent local chapter of the American Association of Law Librarians or the Special Library Association. The boards of these groups are always looking for new leaders. It looks great on your résumé and helps you get a job later."

"There are lots of opportunities to manage different projects, at least in academic libraries," observed Ann Ercelawn. "There are lots of opportunities as well to observe which supervisors are effective and which are not— take notes on which strategies work and which do not."

Be willing to participate in everything, whether or not you enjoy the task. For example, let's say your department is shorthanded and you are asked to work weekends or extra hours at a reference desk. Maybe your library is asking for volunteers to help with a barcoding project. Volunteer as much as you can, and show that you are willing to do what's needed. A good leader participates alongside his or her employees, with enthusiasm.

"Develop strategy and vision for how to develop yourself," urged Jim Walther. "Look at personal, social, community, and other areas for leadership skills—gain skills through involvement other than work, and list that on your résumé. What skills do you want? How can you use volunteer opportunities to build those skills? Only 9 percent of nonmanagers are given leadership training through work." Be creative when finding ways to build your leadership skills.

"Volunteer to take charge of any one-time projects that aren't addressed by any standing committee or department," advised Michelle Mach. "For example, I volunteered for a two-person task force assigned to investigate in-house librarian awards. One-time projects are great because they have a finite time frame and give you a concrete accomplishment to show for your work. Depending upon the structure and size of the library, it may be a while before you can participate in a standing committee and these smaller projects allow you to demonstrate leadership in the meantime. Student organizations like honor societies or ethnic associations on campus are often eager for active staff and faculty participation. Because they are often smaller and less formal in structure, they usually offer more opportunities for leadership for new members than more traditional university committees."

Ann Green said, "When I moved from D.C. to Wisconsin to work in a one-person library, I joined the Wisconsin chapter of AALL (LLAW) in order to meet people and get out of my own library occasionally. That led to being president of the chapter eventually!"

"Learn leadership skills by supervising student workers or serving on smaller committees or task forces, especially as chair," said Marcia Keyser. "For example, we had an Anti-Noise Task Force. Volunteer in smaller library (or other) professional organizations that need people to do things. The Texas Library Association has always been happy to put me to work. Also, volunteering in nonlibrary organizations can sometimes give you relevant experience."

Angela Horne described how library school helped her develop leadership skills. "Library school was the catalyst, prodding students to participate on team projects that weren't always led well. This caused the more conscientious amongst us to shoulder more of the responsibilities for meeting deadlines and organizing tasks."

"One of the best ways I can think of is to become involved in committee work within your library," advised Richard Murray. "Most libraries always seem to be looking for people who are actually interested in serving on committees so that they don't have to recruit people against their will and stick them on a committee they have no desire to be on. Even if you're just serving on a committee rather than chairing it, you'll learn a lot about leadership by watching the chair. If he or she is a good leader, you'll see skills and behaviors you might want to practice. If he or she is a bad leader, you'll see behaviors you'll want to avoid (and the problems that result if you don't). I've always believed you can learn as much from failure—whether it's your own or somebody else's—as you can from success. Learning what not to do is just as important as learning what to do.

"The other great thing about serving on committees within your library is that it's often the best way to meet people who work in other divisions of your organization who you might otherwise never get a chance to work with. This can be especially important if you're working in a really large environment, such as a big university library. Besides the inevitable 'networking is good' result," concluded Murray, "starting to meet and interact with people in other divisions will give you a better idea of the big picture in your library, and also maybe help you understand why things work the way they do in your organization (for better or for worse)."

Sometimes you may become leader of a group or task accidentally—for example, when the chair resigns unexpectedly. If you keep the project moving ahead, your supervisors and others will appreciate your taking control in a crisis and will recognize your leadership potential.

Marcia Keyser described her accidental leadership development experience "being a member of a two-member task force in which the other person's mother developed a chronic illness—hence, I was the only active member! Of course you can't make something like this happen, but when life suddenly throws in such curves, be forthcoming and helpful and the opportunity to gain skills could emerge."

"From personal experience," added Richard Murray, "I can say that sometimes leadership roles are thrust upon you whether you ask for them or not. About four months after I started at my current job—my first professional position—I was asked (i.e., told) to chair a committee that was to decide whether the library was going to spend tens of thousands of dollars on a project. As any sensible person would be, I was petrified. I was new to the organization, didn't know a lot of what was going on, and didn't know the people I was working with that well. I know it sounds trite, but you sink or swim. You make mistakes, you accept them, fix whatever damage you may have caused, and move on. Don't be afraid to ask questions or admit when you need advice; they don't expect you to know everything. The important thing is to appear confident, whether you really feel it or not. Chances are, they wouldn't have asked you to assume the role if they didn't believe you could do it; as tempting as it may be to feel otherwise, most people don't enjoy seeing others fail. Take what you're given and run with it. Being given a leadership role in that case was one of the best things that's ever happened to me, even though at the time I wondered what I'd done to deserve such punishment."

Project Management

Organize yourself and your work area so that you can keep track of projects. If you agree to take on a project—whether it's an assignment at work, a volunteer opportunity, a committee appointment within an organization— fulfill your responsibility. Accomplish the task by the deadline. Let others involved know what you're doing. You'll quickly build a reputation as someone who does things, someone who carries through what you promise to do.

When leading a team or project, ask for assistance but clearly explain who's going to do what. Follow up on who's done what and who hasn't. Get feedback. Emphasize the teamwork needed to accomplish the goal; project the idea that "we're all in this together." Allow or ensure that people can walk away if they begin to get burned out or overwhelmed. Look at what goes wrong to see how to improve.

Communicate constantly. Collaborate. Ask open-ended questions. Start projects on timelines and give constant feedback to your teammates or committee members.

Communication

Communicate regularly with your supervisors, coworkers, and employees. Be sure everyone is in the loop. Be sure people know what you're doing, and ask for help when necessary. Don't be afraid to ask your boss for guidance. Get input from coworkers, employees, vendors, and others. Develop good listening skills. Listen to others' ideas and let them know you appreciate hearing from them. Develop your oral and written communication skills so that you can write reports or present your case effectively. Keep your supervisors and others well informed of your work so that they recognize what you're doing. A bit of self-promotion is necessary so that your supervisors or others in a position to give you opportunities will know that you are active. Remember to back up your words with actions—if you say you'll do something, or did something, make sure you have or will follow through. In committee work, especially when you are working with teams that work primarily by e-mail, be sure to keep in touch with everyone. When you don't meet face-to-face regularly, others have no way to know that you're working on the committee's projects. This also helps keep your name in the top of their minds, when they are looking for a chair or leader down the road.

Leading from Nonsupervisory Positions

"Observe those who supervise you," encouraged Judy Albert. "See what works and what doesn't. Consider how particular styles or methods of decision making affect your work. Examine your own capabilities as a leader—is a supervisory position right for you? Not everyone is cut out to be a manager, and there is nothing worse than for someone who isn't, to aspire to that level, often for the wrong reasons (money comes to mind), and not realize his/her shortcomings."

Bob Schatz added, "Develop and maintain respect for other people, no matter what their position. Good leaders respect those who report to them, and to whom they report. Pay attention to those attributes that you respect most in the people to whom you report. Believe in yourself, and in your ability to be fair to others. Realize that great leaders are in it for the people they lead, not for themselves."

"Learn by example," urged Alison Hopkins. "I learned by watching others, learning from what I agreed with and what I thought could have been handled better. I would run through situations in my mind, decide what I would have done, and watch another person—I then added to my knowledge base. This was especially useful when learning how to handle customer situations. I would try to handle them myself, then call a supervisor, and see how they resolved the situation."

"How you define supervisory skills is the key," Laura Sill reflected. "Supervisory skills run the spectrum from communication, organizational, personnel management, planning, leadership, etc. I think even when you are not in a supervisory role, you can work on developing skills that would assist you in a supervisory position. For example, you can show leadership on projects, committees, within your work group, etc. You can work on your relationships with your colleagues as a way to develop personnel management skills (i.e., interpersonal skills)."

Gerald Clark said, "You can demonstrate leadership even when not in a supervisory position. Leadership includes being proactive rather than reactive. Leadership means having all your 'staff work' done before presenting something to your supervisor (for review, for approval, etc.); this includes keeping up with advances in your field. Leadership means bringing your supervisor solutions, not problems. These are things I learned from twenty years' work in the USDA-Forest Service, before I became a librarian."

"Observe and model others that you feel are good leaders," advised Susan Davis. "Demonstrate competence and interest in the assignment that you have. Become involved with committees, task forces, student organizations, etc. Volunteer for an assignment and then do a great job with it! And learn to listen."

Supervising Others

Encourage, recognize, and reward others for their accomplishments. If you are in a supervisory position, take every opportunity to encourage and thank those who work for you whenever they've accomplished something special or worked overtime or gone out of their way to fix a problem. Recognize their achievements and efforts as publicly as possible—maybe in a meeting or with a thank-you letter or newsletter. If you're able, reward them with good evaluations or merit raises. If you're not able to do that, find creative ways to reward innovative ideas and consistent production. People want to be recognized for their work, even if you're recognizing the fact that they come to work on time every day; or are very accurate in their work; etc.

If you're supervising other employees, use this as a learning opportunity. Watch other supervisors and take advantage of training when you can. Be approachable. Participate; learn what your employees do so that you really understand what they do. Be alert to potential problems. Give employees constant feedback so that they know how they're doing, whether they're meeting expectations, etc. Remember to give positive feedback as well as negative.

Empower employees to do their best. Remove obstacles that hamper them from doing their best. Delegate as much as possible and give employees the authority to make decisions. Give them as much leeway to take initiative as you can, while still being available to guide them. This doesn't mean you just leave them to flounder and expect that they will come to you when they have questions. Some will, but many won't. Achieving a balance between guiding and delegating is very difficult. Micromanaging can hamper creativity and enthusiasm; your employees may come up with great ideas and you should encourage them. Be alert to what they're doing so that you can correct mistakes or guide them if they are feeling overwhelmed or confused.

Laura Sill said, "When moving into a supervisory role, make clear what your new roles are, but always emphasize that your work relationship is peer-based. I think this is one of the trickiest situations in which to find yourself. You must have respect for new roles (for example, you—as the manager—may need to make decisions or make the final call on situations). Reflect on the value and expertise that the person you are now supervising brings to your operation. I think this goes a long ways to reminding you of their skills, but also gives them a sense that they are valued and not less now in terms of your working relationship."

Try to focus on people rather than production or ego or statistics or whatever. How can you help others achieve their best? Give them information so that they can do their job. Encourage and reward them. Try to explain things in such a way that employees will buy into a project and understand why they are doing what they're doing. Show them that you're doing it along with them and make them feel part of the overall mission or goal of the organization.

When you become a manager, don't forget to manage (as well as do your own job). You were probably promoted because you knew how to do your job well, but now you have to manage others. If you are managing people you used to work with, this can cause problems. Be firm. Set goals and objectives for your staff, give clear directions, and let them go at it. Correct them in private but praise them in public. The time you spend seeing how your new staff is doing and showing them how to do something better makes everyone more efficient. It may feel easier to do things yourself rather than taking time to show others how to do things— in fact, most new managers do this. Learn to delegate. This is an important learning experience for you and them. Get advice from mentors.

You can't control everything. Some people won't want to work as hard as you want. You can't manage your staff into being smarter or more hard-working than they are. Don't be afraid to fire someone if you have to.

Supervising Peers

What if you're managing someone who is at your level—a team of librarians, for example? Create a collegial team environment, encouraged Beverley Geer. "My job [as a manager] is to make sure people who report to me have everything they need to do their job effectively," she explained. "Treat everyone with regard and respect. Don't hover. Let others know where they stand."

"Consistent behavior is very important," added Bob Schatz. "Employees shouldn't have to wonder or fear what mood you're in. I call my management style 'participatory dictatorship' because I'm the one who ultimately is held responsible. Get input but ultimately make hard decisions. Conduct yourself in a way that employees will respect you and don't worry about whether they like you."

You work for your employees as an advocate; usually they will understand and respect you. "To manage" is an active verb—don't be reactive and wait for things to happen. Establish relationships (manager vs. friend) right away and be consistent. Explain why you made a decision; help others understand the reasoning behind your decisions.

Bob Schatz advised, "When you supervise someone you used to work with as a peer, treat them the same as you would anyone else you supervise. Be fair, be firm, be consistent, give lots of feedback, and maintain a sense of humor. Understand your own weaknesses, and don't try to pretend to employees that you think you have no weaknesses."

REFLECTIONS ON LEADERSHIP

"I never considered myself a leader and didn't really want a position of serious responsibility," reflected Jean Hirons. "But when Linda Bartley announced that she was leaving, I realized that I had a rare opportunity to take on a job of great significance. But I couldn't do what Linda did. I had to find my own way of leading CONSER. So I did what came naturally. I concentrated on the documentation and started a training program! I also fought for the single record option for electronic versions as a commonsense approach to dealing with a growing problem and have taken on a number of other issues that make me quite nervous. But I have never failed to be surprised at how popular some of my ideas have been, even though they may not be as popular here at LC. I've learned that if I think something is a good idea, I need to stick to it and trust myself. I am very fortunate, however, in having a broad network of friends in the serials community with whom I can discuss new ideas. Having their support boosts my own confidence and ability to push for something that I believe in. So in terms of leadership, I believe that you have to be true to yourself and trust your own instincts when making decisions and proposing new ideas. But also find a group of trusted friends to help you out! None of us are in this alone."

Barbara Allen (director, Center for Institutional Cooperation) wrote: In thinking about my own leadership style or philosophy, I chose to focus not so much on what makes a great leader, but to look at the other side of the coin for clues. My assistant director, Russ Snyder, is fond of saying that nothing is ever a total failure—it can always serve as a bad example. All of us have worked for spectacularly incompetent bosses at one time or another. These people are the anti-leaders. Believing that it is as important to know what I hope not to be as to know what I hope to become, I've developed the following quick list of the seven habits of the highly ineffectual anti-leader:

7. They are soulless. Put them in charge of a college, a health clinic, or an Orange Julius. It doesn't matter to them. They have no connection to their work.
6. They are emotional black holes sucking the life force from those around them. These people are threatened by competence in others and choose to stomp out creativity.
5. They embarrass you in public. Either through arrogance, ignorance, or stupendously poor personal hygiene, you cringe to imagine them as the public personae of your organization.
4. They are unresponsive. They don't return your phone calls or acknowledge your e-mails. You're not so sure they even read their mail. You are reduced to trying to communicate with them telepathically in a desperate attempt to elicit feedback or direction on your own work.
3. They are inconsistent. They are weather vanes, not polestars.
2. They neither seek nor accept input from staff and constituents.
1. They do not communicate. Within or outside the organization.

"Beware," Allen cautioned. "Do not be one of these people. Rather, strive for humility and deep humanity in your undertakings. Cultivate a great curiosity and hunger for understanding and learning. Believe in the beauty and importance of your work, and develop an unwavering commitment and will to succeed. Then convey that commitment and integrity to your staff."

SUMMARY

- Develop the four personal qualities of a good leader: purpose, trust, optimism, and action.
- Develop integrity in your personal and professional life. Make sure your actions match your words and vision.

- Create an atmosphere of trust by encouraging individual viewpoints and dissent.
- Volunteer to lead special projects, chair committees, and organize events. Use group interactions as an opportunity to work on your leadership skills.
- Improve your project management and communication skills.
- In nonsupervisory positions, learn from your supervisors, both good and bad.
- In supervisory positions, treat others with respect and continue to develop your leadership skills.

RELATED READINGS

Leadership

Beasley, Augie. "Becoming a Proactive Library Leader: Leadership 101." *School Library Media Activities Monthly* 13 (November 1996): 20–2.

Bennis, Warren, and Joan Goldsmith. *Learning to Lead: A Workbook on Becoming a Leader*. Reading, Mass.: Perseus Books, 1997. Recommended by Maureen Sullivan at the ALA New Members Round Table Preconference, "Learning to Lead," July 2000.

Berry, John N. "Leadership Liberates." *Library Journal* 123, no. 15 (15 September 1998): 6.

Bowlby, Raynna. "Learning to Lead: It's Not Just in Classrooms Anymore!" *College & Research Libraries News* 60, no. 4 (April 1999): 292–3.

Covey, Stephen R. *Principle-Centered Leadership*. London: Simon & Schuster, 1991.

Deiss, Kathryn J. "Personal Best: the Continuous Process of Learning to Be a Self-Leader." *College & Research Libraries News* 60, no. 3 (March 1999): 193–4.

Dowell, David R. "Leadership: In the Eye of the Beholder?" In *Leadership and Academic Librarians*. Westport, Conn.: Greenwood Press, 1998.

Flowers, Janet L. "Developing Excellence in Leadership and Followership: A Bibliographic Essay." *North Carolina Libraries* 54 (summer 1996): 68–73.

Glendenning, Barbara J. "Professional Associations: Promoting Leadership in a Career." *Library Trends* 46, no. 2 (fall 1997): 258–77.

Hurlbert, Janet McNeil. "Every Instructional Services Librarian a Leader: Leadership in the Small Academic Library." In *Leadership and Academic Librarians*, edited by Terrence F. Mech. Westport, Conn.: Greenwood Press, 1998.

"Learning to Lead." *The School Librarian's Workshop* 11 (June 1991): 1–2.

Newman, George Charles. "Leading from Within: Leadership within the Ranks of Academic Librarians." In *Leadership and Academic Librarians*, edited by Terrence F. Mech. Westport, Conn.: Greenwood Press, 1998.

Quinn, Brian A. "Librarians' and Psychologists' View of Leadership: Converging and Diverging Perspectives." *Library Administration & Management* 13, no. 3 (summer 1999): 147–57.

Reynolds, Judy. "There Must Be 50 Ways to Be a Leader." *College & Research Libraries News,* no. 4 (April 1996): 208–10.

St. Lifer, Evan. "Prime Leadership." *Library Journal* 123, no. 15 (15 September 1998): 36–8.

Schill, Victor. "Sowing the Seeds of Leadership." *Texas Library Journal* 73, no. 3 (fall 1997): 122–3.

Sheldon, Brooke E. "Leadership in the Workplace." *Texas Library Journal* 75, no. 4 (winter 1999): 142.

Spies, Phyllis Bova. "Libraries, Leadership, and the Future." *Library Management* 21, no. 3 (2000): 123–7.

Sullivan, Maureen. "Leadership through the Lens of Learning: A Look at the Role of the Librarian for the New Century." *College & Research Libraries News* 59, no. 9 (October 1998): 673–4.

Sweeney, Patricia James. "The Librarian As Leader." *Catholic Library World* 70, no. 2 (December 1999): 98–103.

Supervising

Anderson, Arthur James. "Nobody Told Me How." *Library Journal* 112 (15 June 1987): 50–3.

Baldwin, David A. *Supervising Student Employees in Academic Libraries*. Englewood, Colo.: Libraries Unlimited, 1991.

Banks, Julie. "A Practicum: Views of Two Supervising Librarians." *Journal of Education for Library and Information Science* 33 (summer 1992): 241–7.

Beasley, Augie. "Leadership 101: Survival Skills for School/Media Coordinators." *North Carolina Libraries* 54 (summer 1996): 54–7.

Blenkinsopp, Heather. "Communicating across Cultures for Reference Librarians Who Supervise." *The Reference Librarian* no. 45–46 (1994): 39–43.

Burek, Ann. "One Person's View of Supervising Paraprofessionals." *Colorado Libraries* 26, no. 1 (spring 2000): 25–6.

Cochrane, John. "Be a Better Supervisor with Behaviour Management." *New Zealand Libraries* 45 (December 1987): 177–9.

Fitzmaurice, Ann M. "Training for Leadership." *Library Trends* 40 (winter 1992): 543–52.

Giesecke, Joan, ed. *Practical Help for New Supervisors*. Chicago, Ill.: American Library Association, 1997.

Henderson, Pat. "What Do You Mean, I'm in Charge of Serials?" *Library Collections, Acquisitions and Technical Services* 23, no. 1 (spring 1999): 126–7.

"Managers: Use These Strategies to Help Employees Manage Their Careers." *Library Personnel News* 13, no. 1–2 (spring/summer 2000): 9.

Newman, George Charles. "Becoming an Effective Academic Library Manager: Preparation, Process, and Performance." *Library Administration & Management* 4 (winter 1990): 33–7.

"Once You Master the Hiring Process, You May Never Have to Fire Anyone Again." *Library Personnel News* 13, no. 1–2 (spring/summer 2000): 13–14.

Piccininni, James C. "Advice for First-Time Library Directors on Managing a Library." *Library Administration & Management* 10 (winter 1996): 41–3.

Plas, Jeanne. "Discover What Matters Most to Employees." *Library Personnel News* 13, no. 1–2 (spring/summer 2000): 3.

Rogers, Shelley L. "Out of Theory and into Practice: Supervising Library Employees." *The Journal of Academic Librarianship* 19 (July 1993): 154–7.

"Supervising Teens." *The Unabashed Librarian,* no. 80 (1991): 14.

Wallace, Virginia L. "Supervising the High School Library Media Center Internship." *Book Report* 18, no. 2 (September/October 1999): 28–30.

Walton, Stephanie. "The Benefits of Supervising: The Unsung Role of Paralibrarians." *Colorado Libraries* 21 (spring 1995): 42–3.

CHAPTER 8

Writing and Publishing

Woo-hoo! Who woulda guessed reading and writing would pay off!

—Homer Simpson, *The Simpsons*

I once asked this literary agent what writing paid the best, and he said, "ransom notes."

—Harry Zimm, *Get Shorty* (1995)

Why should you publish? For many academic librarians, publication is a requirement to earn tenure and promotion. However, professional publication has many other rewards. You do research to increase your own knowledge, which broadens your knowledge base, which in turn can help you in your job. You enhance your professional self-worth. You make a name for yourself, particularly in your field of research. Publishing can gain you professional recognition or career advancement. You come in contact with other library leaders and widen your network in doing your research or interviews. You contribute to the good of the information profession, serve other professionals in the field, and contribute to the literature used by others in the field. If you work with academic clientele, you can become more aware of the problems facing them as scholars. You gain personal satisfaction from meeting your goals, developing writing skills, and achieving personal goals. Sometimes, you even earn royalties.

PLACES TO PUBLISH

The most common places to publish are a journal or a book. If you find the thought of writing a journal article daunting, try writing book reviews or newsletter articles, recording conference proceedings, compiling bibliographies, writing letters to the editor, and so on, to build your confidence and gain writing experience. Also, consider writing for electronic journals or

Web sites. Articles get published in electronic journals much more quickly than in print journals or books.

If you are publishing in order to get tenure or promotion, ask your employer for their expectations and guidelines. When reviewing your performance for tenure or promotion, some institutions consider only publications in peer-reviewed, scholarly journals or books, while other organizations have more lenient guidelines for publication.

There are other ways to break into publishing—for example, becoming involved in focus groups, advisory boards, editorial boards, prepublication reviews and committees. Volunteering experience can lead to contacts and potential opportunities.

Bob Schatz reflected, "My first item of publication was a two-page thought piece, born of being irritated at a growing number of publishers who kept cutting vendor discounts. I wrote it in one draft and got it accepted for publication in the first journal to which I submitted it. It came from the heart, usually a good source for meaningful writing."

"I still remember the thrill of getting my first article accepted over thirty years ago," wrote Robert Holley (interim dean, University Libraries, Wayne State University), former senior co-editor of the journal, *Resource Sharing and Information Networks*. "Our journal is looking for all kinds of articles in the area of resource sharing and information networks as very broadly defined. I've edited the journal for a long time and worked closely with authors to bring their manuscripts up to the standards required by my reviewers. Manuscript should be in the range of about eight to thirty-five double-spaced pages.

"We also look for book reviewers," encouraged Holley. "Many new writers find this an easier task because the book gives them focus. I look for substantive reviews of at least five double-spaced pages. The review should not only give the contents of the book but should also include evaluative comments by the reviewer. As I look across my office, I see at least fifteen books that await reviewers. My one caution is that you keep your promise if you agree to review the book because I've promised publishers a review in return for sending the book. As a reward for writing the review, you get to keep the book. You can take several months to write the review, as long as I know that you'll eventually complete it."

"I don't know how much reviewing helps you get your foot in the door as far as other writing," commented Rachel Singer Gordon, "but it can help in related areas. I've been reviewing for *Library Journal* for the last couple of years, and it's helped my writing become more concise (their reviews are generally limited to 150 words). Also, during the last couple of job interviews I have been on, the interviewer specifically mentioned my being an *LJ* reviewer and seemed favorably impressed. It's a good thing to be able to put on your résumé. Also, writing longer reviews may be seen more as an article credit than would writing shorter ones such as in *LJ*."

Anne Tomlin (medical librarian, Auburn Memorial Hospital) said, "I started writing abstracts about ten years ago and it was so neat to see my name in print, and contribute to my profession, that I applied to be a book reviewer for *Library Journal*, which I've been doing ever since. My first freelance article was written out of frustration and sent off—with no real expectation of publication—to *The One-Person Library*, then owned and edited by Guy St. Clair, bless him, who not only published my article on solos and absenteeism, but paid me for it and encouraged me to write again. I did, eventually becoming an editorial advisor for the newsletter. It's now owned by Judith Siess and I serve on its board of correspondents, writing the occasional article or report. I also wrote an article for *Marketing Library Services* and the *Medical Reference Services Quarterly*. About five years ago, I took on a quarterly column on one-person libraries for *National Network*, the newsletter for the Hospital Libraries section of the Medical Library Association. This past year I have been appointed research column editor for a forthcoming journal from Haworth Press, *The Journal of Hospital Librarianship*. On the side, so to speak, I write a quarterly column for *First Draft* on Internet resources for mystery writers. So from little acorns . . . I may not be a mighty oak but a thriving sapling? Reviewing is a great way to get your toes wet," encouraged Tomlin. "Go for it!"

JOURNAL PUBLISHING

Generate Ideas

First, you have to get an idea. How do you do this? Brainstorm with yourself and with others. Ask yourself, "What interests me? What do I do well? What would I like to read? What interests people around me?" Talk to your colleagues and to the public to find out what topics interest them.

Find associations that support your interests, and begin communicating with others in that association through e-mail, committee involvement, and so on. Attend professional meetings; maybe a presentation or a conversation will spark an idea. Volunteer to speak at meetings; sometimes your research for your presentation, or the questions that your audience asks you, can develop into a publication. Write authors of articles that you read and enjoy; sometimes this may lead to coauthorship opportunities or other ideas.

Alison Hopkins commented, "The two articles I published were based on poster sessions I did at ALA. I was on a committee at work. We presented two poster sessions and were approached by journal editors at ALA to ask us to write them up for publication. Both articles were published, one in *The Reference Librarian* and one in *The Unabashed Librarian*."

"I have a somewhat different approach that seems to work well—for me, anyway," said Angelynn King (reference and bibliographic instruction librarian, University of Redlands). "I propose presentations to conferences large and small, and the ones that I actually end up doing serve as good outlines for papers. When I send out queries, I've already done the presentation, so I have a pretty good idea of what I will say—but I don't write the actual article until it's accepted somewhere. For the most part, my experiences have been positive; with presentations, as with publications, the trick is finding the proper forum for the idea you already have."

Reading professional journals regularly can help generate ideas. Also, read journals or literature in other fields. You might decide to publish in a nonlibrary journal, or you may apply research from another field to a problem or issue in our field. Jot down your ideas or keep an "ideas file." File articles that interest you. Periodically revisit your file to see if an idea hits you in a new light.

When you have an idea, search the literature to familiarize yourself with what's published and to see whether the topic has been exhausted. Try to find a fresh approach to topics so that you don't duplicate what's already been written. Ask colleagues or mentors for their opinions about your ideas.

"Do some research," encouraged Wayne Jones. "Make sure you are not writing about something that has already been covered in the literature. Contact the editors of professional journals with ideas, or with an actual full article you have written—yes, just go ahead and submit something! In the article, make sure you have the formalities right. Use correct style and footnoting, for example. And an obvious piece of advice that is not so obvious: make sure the writing is good, free of jargon, not trashy and colloquial, but clean and clear while at the same time professional. My first article," he remembered, "came about when the editor of a professional journal contacted my institution asking for an article on a certain subject. A coworker and I wrote it."

Rachel Singer Gordon said, "In your own professional reading, look for gaps in the literature. What seems as if it's missing? What do you wish other authors had expanded on? What would you like to learn more about?

Also, don't hold back from submitting an idea because you don't feel as if you are an expert on the subject. You're a librarian—you can research it!"

Marcia Keyser suggested, "If you've got an idea but aren't sure whether it is worth writing about, ask yourself this: If someone else wrote and published this, would it be a helpful article to you? Why or why not? Next, if it is something that would help you (or that you are interested in), assume that it would help or interest other librarians in similar jobs."

Analyze Audience and Publications

Notice which journals have published articles about your topic. Identify potential places to publish. Read a journal's "Instructions for Authors" to see what submission requirements the journal has. Ask colleagues to suggest appropriate journals for your article.

Analyze publications. For example, find out what subjects are covered, what approach or writing style is used, whether there is a geographical or occupational slant, whether articles are contributed by freelancers or by the publisher's staff, and how long the articles are. Use the Internet to find ideas or possible publishing avenues, such as electronic library journals. Table 8.1 lists a few guides to publications. Nesbeitt and Gordon's book, *The Information Professional's Guide to Career Development Online*, includes a detailed list of publishing outlets. In table 8.2, former *Serials Review* editor Cindy Hepfer shares some guidelines for choosing a publisher.

Table 8.1   On-line Guides to Publications

Publist.com: an Internet Directory of Publications
    http://www.publist.com.

Index Morganagus: A Full-Text Index of Library-Related Electronic Serials
    http://sunsite.berkeley.edu/~emorgan/morganagus/

Serials Publications: Resources for Authors
    http://www.nasig.org/publications/pub_resources.html

Finding Professional Literature on the Net
    http://www.lib.umich.edu/libhome/ILSL.lib/literature.html

ALA Periodicals List
    http://www.ala.org/library/alaperiodicals.html

BUBL List of Library and Information Science Journals
    http://bubl.ac.uk/journals/lis/

LibraryHQ List of Library and Information Science Publishers
    http://www.libraryhq.com/publishers.html

Table 8.2   Guidelines for Choosing a Publisher

When preparing an article for publication, consider the following when deciding where to submit a manuscript:

- Do I want to publish in a library journal or one that is discipline-related?
- Does the journal that I aspire to publish and carry articles in my field of interest?
- Does the journal publish the type of article (research paper, case study, etc.) that I want to write?
- Does the journal publish frequent special/theme issues which I might be part of?
- What is the journal's reputation/prestige/impact factor?
- Where is the journal indexed—and is it widely indexed?
- Am I willing to publish my work in an Internet-based journal, as opposed to one that is available in print? What are the benefits/drawbacks of publishing in an on-line only journal?
- Is the journal scholarly/research or practitioner-oriented? What size and level of audience does it have?
- Is the journal peer-reviewed? If the answer is yes, then what kind of peer-review process is undertaken (blinded/double blinded)? Who makes the final decision to accept/reject?
- Are invited articles subjected to peer-review?
- What is the journal's rejection/acceptance rate?
- Will the editor provide me with constructive criticism and an opportunity to revise the paper?
- Am I willing to spend the time to revise my paper if an editor says it is necessary?
- Is the journal the official organ of a particular organization? If so, must authors be members of the organization to be published in the journal?
- How long are the articles or contributions in a particular journal, on average?
- If I want to include illustrations of any kind with my paper, how well can the journal reproduce them?
- Which style manual does the editor follow?
- Are there author guidelines in the publication or mounted on the Web, or can the editor provide me with a copy?
- What kind of copyright agreement will I be expected to sign if my article is accepted for publication? Will I retain any rights to the paper?
- Does the journal have page charges that I must pay?
- Will the editor acknowledge receipt of my manuscript?
- On average, how long will I have to wait to find out whether my manuscript has been accepted for publication?
- What is the frequency of publication, and how long will it take for my article to get into print after it is accepted?
- Will I get to review proofs of the paper and make necessary changes? And if the paper has been in a publication queue for some time, will I be permitted to update the paper when I see the proofs? Will the publisher charge me for such revisions at the proof stage?
- Will the publisher provide me with a free copy of the issue in which my article is published? Will reprints be provided, and can I purchase extra reprints?

Source: Hepfer, Cindy (head, Collection Management Services, Health Sciences Library, State University of New York at Buffalo). "Getting Published." Presentation to SLA Student Chapter, SUNY Buffalo (9 October 1999).

"I was just reading *Library Journal* one day," reminisced Sarah Nesbeitt, "when I saw a blurb asking librarians with experience evaluating Internet resources to consider writing a Web Watch column. I contacted the editor, submitted a writing sample and some ideas, and he gave me a deadline—I believe this was back in 1997. The topic was 'on-line phone and address directories,' which I thought of because we were getting numerous questions about this at the reference desk, and we were considering canceling our subscription to PhoneDisc in favor of one of the Internet phone directories. I wrote a second Web Watch column for *LJ* several months later. As it turned out, another librarian who runs a library employment Web site, Rachel Gordon, had written three columns for Norman Oder at *LJ* as well. We'd been sending e-mail messages back and forth about library careers and employment, and eventually we decided to coauthor an article in which we surveyed librarians about their career paths. At that point, we weren't sure who would publish it, but after it was done, we told Norman about it. He asked us to fax him a copy. He showed it to another editor there, and as it turns out, they decided to publish it as the cover story (May 15, 1999).

"I would say that if you're just starting out, look for those 'calls for reviewers' that appear in various publications, and contact an editor that way. That's how I got my start writing columns for *LJ*," continued Nesbeitt. "I've seen similar requests for various journals. These editors are actually asking for people to submit articles to them, so why not take advantage of this? This can be less intimidating than sending a completely unsolicited article in to a publication. If a person's got good ideas and can write, I don't see any reason why she or he shouldn't aim for one of the big journals first. It's a really good boost to one's career. If someone needs to gain some writing experience first, though, there's always the statewide library journal/newsletter. Many of these have very high acceptance rates, so there's a better chance that what you submit will be published. In addition, there's plenty of opportunity for people to get some experience with book or Web site reviewing in publications such as *LJ*, *Choice*, or my own journal, *Electronic Resources Review*. Around half of the reviewers whom I've found through my recent call for reviewers don't have any previous publishing experience, and many are turning out to be quite good writers."

Kerry Smith (library instruction services coordinator, Mississippi State University Libraries) reflected, "To date, I've had two articles accepted in writing and one accepted verbally (and two rejected—one with helpful comments, one without). The following may not be the best or wisest approach, but each time I've written the article first, on a topic that interested me. I then looked at the journals available and matched the article to potentially interested journals whose tone and style were similar to my article (since I'm in a tenure-track position, I lean heavily toward peer-reviewed journals, but it depends on the tone of the article). I then ranked the journals in terms of where I wanted most to publish (a variety of factors can influence this), read carefully the first journal's guidelines for authors and the required style format, and then modified the article to fit. Then I submitted the article, along with a brief cover letter, and waited the customary six to eight weeks, if I had to, before querying the editor regarding the manuscript. If rejected, I repeat the process down through my ranked journals list. So far, most of the editors have replied relatively quickly, with helpful comments, and have been great at assisting the paper toward publication. Editors want to publish good stuff, and overall they seem to be willing to work heavily with promising papers and authors. So far, I've had fairly good luck at being accepted by the first or second journal I submit to. That luck may be due to my journal selection process, during which I read the author's guidelines, look at past issues or tables of contents, and read some articles from a recent issue of the journal."

Select an audience for your article. Write your article or publication to that audience. Some authors recommend visualizing a specific reader as you write, so that you keep the article focused at your specific audience. This may help keep your writing style consistent and may ensure that you cover details that are important to your readers.

Write a Query Letter and Abstract

Develop a brief outline or abstract for your article. If you are writing a research article, develop your goals, objectives, and methodology for your study. Begin gathering information for your article through research, reading, interviewing, or surveying others.

You may wish to write a query letter to assess the journal editor's interest. Follow any guidelines stated in the journal's "Instructions to Authors." A query letter should demonstrate your best writing. Include a concise summary of your proposal and your qualifications, and request that the editor consider your completed manuscript. You may want to send query letters before beginning your writing, but you can also do so to find a publisher for a completed article.

It can take several months to hear from an editor, although editors will often respond immediately to let you know they have received your query letter or your article. They will usually give you an estimated timeline for acceptance. If you have had no response after about one month, write or call the editor to ask if he or she received your query letter or article. If you still hear nothing, send the letter or article to another publisher, and let the first publisher know that you have done so.

"There are two ways of finding a journal," offered Ann Grafstein (reference librarian and circulation coordinator, College of Staten Island/CUNY). "You can pick some place you wanted to submit it to. That's what I generally do. You might look at the journals that the sources you cite were published in. Or search Ulrich's for journals that publish similar articles (there doesn't need to be an exact match). I've also just browsed through journals that are in my library to see which ones might be amenable. Some people find it more efficient to send an abstract of a written article—or a letter proposing an article on a specific topic—around to a several journals to see if they might be interested in publishing an article of that nature. But regardless of what you do, some rejection is, unfortunately, as much a part of the process as death is part of the life cycle.

"The other thing you should do," continued Grafstein, "is to have someone you trust edit the article before you submit it. It's important to select the person carefully. Don't just give it to someone who will tell you what they think you want to hear. Give it to someone who can critically evaluate it for argumentation, organization, and writing style. Good luck and don't—at least try not to—get discouraged."

Janet O'Keefe (team librarian, Flint Public Library) wrote, "Just last night I received a copy of my first professional publication in the mail. Well, it might have been my second, technically. A song parody I wrote with my sister was published between the time this article was accepted, so I'm not sure where it counts. The experience is still pretty fresh in my mind, so I'll let you in on it.

"I wrote the article because I was bored at work and I needed a project, honestly. I had just started a new job and I hadn't gotten into the swing of committee work and my collection development yet. We had four hours off desk a day, which is way too much in my opinion, and I didn't think I was occupied enough. My sister suggested I write an article. To back up a little, I should tell you that I have been studying vampire myths since I was in high school. I have written one book on the subject, but it's been sitting in a drawer since it got rejected by a publisher in my senior year of college. I don't think that counts as sulking, since the only criticism the editor gave me was that it needed to be three times longer. As it was returned to me a week before the first segment of my senior thesis was due, I just didn't have time to deal with it, and frankly I was a little sick of vampires by the time I finished it. After five years off from vampires, I had just unpacked all of my vampire books for the first time since college, and I was willing to address the topic again.

"Whenever I go into a new library," continued O'Keefe, "the first thing I do is check for books on vampires in the OPAC. (Old habits die hard.) I had checked enough OPACs by that time to know that most of the best books on the subjects were no longer in many of the libraries I visited. I had also talked to several librarians in charge of folklore who had no idea what the best books on the topic were. Since most of the best books weren't current, they weren't appearing in reviewing publications either. So I decided to write a guide for purchasing books on vampire myths. It was surprisingly easy for me to get back into the swing of things and write it. I think I spent about a month on it, including having coworkers proofread it and rewrites.

"Since I work in a public library, I assumed my article would be of primary interest to public librarians and I submitted it to *Public Libraries*. They acknowledged receipt of my article immediately, but said they had not received the disk I sent along with it. I e-mailed them another electronic version, and I think it took about two to three months to get a decision. The reviewers had all liked the article and said it was well written, but they said they really didn't publish bibliographies any more. (My first mistake.) The editor suggested I submit it to *RUSQ*. I hadn't thought about *RUSQ* when I wrote it, but I knew the editor had been one of my professors and that she had praised my writing, so I was encouraged. I submitted it to *RUSQ* immediately, and again they didn't get the disk. (I want to know who all these postal disk thieves are!) Again, they said that they all liked the article but that they didn't publish bibliographies. But, they had a column, *The Alert Collector*, that did publish bibliographies and they had forwarded my article to the editor of that column. They gave me her contact information and I e-mailed her, with a fresh copy, that day. She replied immediately and said that she had received the article from *RUSQ* and that she would be getting back with me after she returned from some traveling.

"She accepted the article within, I would say, a month, though I'm not sure. She sent me back the edited copy, but there were very few changes except for the format of the references and basic grammar and spelling. It seemed to take forever for the issue to actually arrive, but it came last night and I am thrilled to bits!" O'Keefe exclaimed.

Write the Article

When an editor expresses interest, begin working immediately if you haven't already done so. Develop a prewriting outline and a timeline for writing. Collect the articles and books you need, and begin your research.

Start writing quickly to avoid blank-screen writer's block. Even if you have to rewrite everything, this may help you not to freeze up. Some authors take notes, then organize the notes according to the outline, and then begin refining those notes into the rough draft. Other authors take notes and formulate the text in their minds before beginning to write. Find the style that works for you, but try to write a little each day or week to stay on track. Write the body first, then the conclusion and introduction. Gather entertaining or illustrative examples, tables, graphs or illustrations to make an article more interesting.

Some writers encourage other writers to keep a journal of what you have done and when it was accomplished, so that you can see progress, particularly if you are doing a long project or doing it in little snatches of time. This can keep your momentum going. Working with others (for example, coauthoring) may help you keep moving on your project. If you find it difficult to keep yourself focused or to meet deadlines, discuss your project with others, ask a friend to help you set a schedule for your writing, or find a writing support group. The NMRTWriter discussion list (table 8.3) was organized by American Library Association New Members Round Table members to provide guidance and support to those interested in publishing.

"In the journal literature, form is somewhat determined by the editor or publisher," Mary Johnson (library director, Missouri Institute of Mental Health), editor of *Behavioral and Social Science Librarian*, recently wrote to aspiring authors on NMRTWriter. "Any prospective author should carefully review—and follow—the guidelines indicated in the section found in

Table 8.3   NMRTWriter

Interested in writing for publication? Check out NMRTWriter.

NMRTWriter is an e-mail discussion group dedicated to supporting librarians looking to write and publish articles, books, grant narratives, or other scholarly communications. We are here to help generate and define topics, discuss the submission process, and share all the tips and hints we can. We encourage experienced as well as novice writers to participate, and welcome librarians from all fields and types of libraries.

NMRTWriter is quite new, but recent contributions have included Web page addresses for the "instruction to authors" sections of various library journals, requests for submissions, and guest commentary from journal editors.

To subscribe, send a message to listproc@ala.org with the following in the body: subscribe nmrtwriter FIRSTNAME LASTNAME Replace both First and Lastname with a real name. Subject line should be empty.

Source: Keyser, Marcia (reference/instruction librarian, Texas A&M University Kingsville). E-mail message to NMRT-L (17 August 2000).

most journals entitled 'information for authors or contributors.' A lot of time and effort is saved if the author has the style elements and cited references in the prescribed format when the manuscript is initially submitted for possible acceptance. If these basics are not heeded, the editor may think that the author either didn't read the journal guidelines, or didn't care enough to follow them. Both suspicions do not set well with editors.

"Authors should familiarize themselves with the specifics of the style required by the journal to which they are submitting their article by obtaining a copy of the appropriate style manual. Commonly used manuals are the *Publication Manual of the American Psychological Association*, the *Chicago Manual of Style*, the *American Medical Association Manual of Style*, the *MLA (Modern Language Association) Style Manual,* and *Guide to Scholarly Publishing*. Access to the basics of several of these editorial styles is now available on the Internet; however, the style manuals themselves provide a wealth of additional information for the writer, including tips on manuscript preparation, discussion of copyright and ethical concerns, reviews of language usage, and much more.

"It is understood that skill in writing varies from person to person. Some people simply are better writers than others are. However, while everyone may not be exceptionally talented in the art of writing, most people have informative things to say and should be heard. Careful crafting and honing of one's material can offset deficiencies in writing style. Grammar and spell-check software makes it easier to create a manuscript devoid of basic language errors, but nothing can take the place of having the proposed article read, reread, and 'red penciled' by a human being. All prospective authors should have their work reviewed by colleagues, both in and out of the library world, to catch grammatical mistakes, to prevent the use of jargon, and to clarify phrasing.

"Content is the other element," continued Johnson. "One should write about something one enjoys and finds interesting. If the topic isn't interesting to the author, it probably won't be interesting to the reader. Writing an article takes a lot of work, and the author should write with the anticipated joy of sharing findings with the larger community because of his or her belief in the value and worth of the research or project the proposed article discusses. However, one needn't undertake massive research to have something to publish. Indeed, the belief that empirical research and theoretical articles are the 'best' kind of articles sometimes causes librarians to think that they don't have anything to contribute. However, many valuable articles come as by-products of some element of day-to-day activities or library routines. The analysis and description of a successful, or not successful, program is a very valuable addition to the literature. Writing about a project your library undertook might give another librarian an idea regarding how to do a similar project or to take your idea and go in another direction.

"Librarians are thought of as information brokers or information mediators or information gatherers—providing access to information produced by others. But in our professional lives, we must also become information generators—creating new work, putting forth new ideas, and adding our voices and experiences to the literature of librarianship."

Edit the Article

When the first draft is written, do a rough edit. Let the first draft cool down before rereading it. Ask yourself, "Is each section vital to the article? Does it flow logically? Have you included enough illustrations or examples? Are the transitions smooth?" You may need to edit and revise it several times in order to get it to flow coherently and smoothly.

After the article has been edited for content and flow, do a more thorough word-by-word editing. Look for unnecessary repetition, unnecessary words, dull verbs, and passive verbs. Edit for clarity. Ask a trusted friend or two to read and comment on your draft. Choose friends who won't just be nice, but will give good constructive criticism

Submit the Final Copy

Prepare a final copy, following the publisher's guidelines explicitly. Make sure the manuscript is neat, with generous margins. Include your name, address, phone number, and number of words in the article. Keep a copy for yourself.

Editors may accept the paper as written, but this is very rare. Don't be surprised or offended if they ask for revisions. In some rare cases, they may reject the publication. If a paper is rejected, edit it if necessary, and send the publication to another publisher.

After an article is accepted for publication, the editor reviews and edits the paper. The editor often sends the article to peer reviewers. Peer reviewers will be asked to answer questions such as: Is the writing style acceptable? Are there major flaws in grammar? Is the article interesting? Is the underlying research sound? Is some major element missing in either subject presentation or format? Should this paper be accepted (with appropriate changes) for publication in this journal?

The author is usually sent a proof copy, and then the article enters the queue for publication. The lag time between acceptance and publication varies with each publication. Sometimes articles will fit into an issue that is being put together, and may appear within a few months. However, it often takes six to eighteen months for an article to appear in print.

Angela Weiler (head of circulation, library instruction coordinator, reference, and Norwich Branch Library coordinator, SUNY Morrisville Library) described her experience publishing a recent article. "Last year I did a survey of students in library instruction sessions on their computer/Internet experiences before coming here. The results were interesting enough to write up, and I finally submitted the article with a cover letter to a highly respected library journal in May. (I figured I'd start at the top and work down!)

"The editor sent me a letter when he received it and told me I'd hear from them in about eight weeks. Sixteen weeks later, I called twice and sent two e-mails to the editor pleading for an answer so I could submit the article to other publications, as the survey data was getting 'cold.' Eventually, he sent back a refusal with the comments from the reviewers, apologizing for what he called their 'lack of tact.' I found their comments to be arrogant bordering on rude, and they gave absolutely no guidance whatsoever for improvement. One comment expressed concerned that I hadn't capitalized 'Internet' in a couple of sentences; another questioned my methodology without any examples or clarification. (Mine was not a formal research study, and I never attempted to give the impression that it was.) In short, this was an extremely negative experience. If I had not already been aware of the wide variety of editorial styles among reviewers from other writing ventures, I might have given up there and then.

"However, I immediately submitted the article (electronically) to two other journals. With one, I was even able to track the progress of my submission on-line, which was a big plus. Both publications accepted the article; I received the first answer and a copy of my article with highly constructive and professional editing suggestions within two weeks, and the second answer came a couple of weeks later. Incidentally, two reviewers from the same publication expressed completely opposite views on the thoroughness of my literature review; I guess sometimes criticism is just a matter of opinion!

Weiler reflected, "It is now clear to me that the first journal accepts only scientific studies which include random sampling, data analysis, etc. However, this was not stated anywhere in their guidelines for submission. This was my first 'cold' submission to a nonfiction publication, although I have written, edited, and published fiction and have had my fiction edited many times. Good editing/reviewing is hard to come by. I realize that most journals use volunteers for the process, but I was surprised to see such a lack of professionalism in reviewing from a top-ranking professional publication."

Kerry Smith commented, "I e-mailed a manuscript once (per author guidelines) and waited the customary six to eight weeks, with no word from the editors. I finally e-mailed a polite note inquiring about the manuscript's status and was told they had no record of that submission and that I should resubmit, which I did. The moral? It doesn't hurt to check."

In her "Getting Published" presentation (see table 8.2), Cindy Hepfer explained her experience editing the journal *Serials Review*. "I receive unsolicited manuscripts," began Hepfer, "but I also solicit specific articles on hot topics or from hot authors. In either case, when I receive a manuscript, I formally acknowledge receipt and give the author a timeline for peer-review and response. I briefly review the paper and decide who should serve as peer-reviewers. I then send the paper, along with a set of instructions, to the individuals I have selected, giving them a deadline of about one month. I often have to follow up with peer-reviewers who do not meet their deadline. It's simply a fact of life that people are very busy and that they can easily let deadlines slip past.

"I carefully read the paper and then look at the feedback that I received from the peer-reviewers. Having formulated an opinion, I then write to the author. My options include: (1) willing to accept/publish as is, but this happens rarely; (2) willing to accept/publish pending specific revisions; (3) willing to reconsider pending (probably fairly substantial) revisions—this may or may not involve another round of peer-review; (4) willing to reconsider if begin all over again, perhaps with a different focus—this will certainly involve another round of peer-review; or (5) reject. Most often, I return the paper asking for minor-to-substantial revisions, and it is not uncommon for me to send a six-to-ten page single spaced letter to an author, along with a manuscript that is marked up with written comments.

"When I receive the revised paper, I once again review it. If it is acceptable, then I do any minor final editing that I believe is required and notify the author that I am accepting the paper for publication. With Pierian Press (the founding publisher), I submitted each article as it was ready. With JAI (who bought the journal from Pierian), I had to send articles for an entire issue all at once. I also had to submit a table of contents, an electronic file of contributors' names and addresses, and my editorial. Elsevier (which bought JAI, including *SR*) will accept the manuscript one article at a time or as an entire issue. However, they require that I fill out a complicated transmission form for each piece. Which issue an article is destined for depends on how many articles I already have in the queue and how long they have been held, whether the topic is one that is very hot or time-dependent, and whether a special issue is in preparation.

"Within a month to six weeks after I submit an issue," continued Hepfer, "the authors and I all receive proof copies. My co-editor and I each review the proofs, along with a retired librarian who has volunteered to proofread. Although I receive proofs back from each author, I generally have to track some of them down. Copyright forms also have to be returned at this stage, having been sent out with proofs from the publisher. Until all of the proofs and copyright forms have been returned, the issue waits; unfortunately, this often takes up to a month.

"The publisher revises the proofs and sends me the revision to review. I compare the new proofs with the first set of proofs, and review heavily edited portions of the proofs from scratch again. Final proofs go only to the managing editor at the publisher. After final corrections, the issue goes to the printer. The printer prints and mails the issues."

BOOK PUBLISHING

Publishing a book is slightly different than publishing an article or shorter work. It's helpful to have some publishing experience behind you to show the publishers. They will usually ask for a writing sample. While most of the advice above also applies to book writing, here are some general steps to publishing a book.

Generate Ideas

Get an idea from reading, from colleagues, from conferences, and so on. Write about something you know a little about already, if possible; but re alize this could be a chance to research a new subject that interests you. Research to see what books have been published on your subject already and compare gaps in coverage. What would be unique about your book?

"Begin by looking around at what you do every day," encouraged Fran Wilkinson. "Is there a problem you have resolved or a project you have led? Check the literature on a topic and if there is something that you would like to know more about, chances are that others would, too. You could start by giving a poster session or a workshop that could develop into an article.

Consider writing your first article with a mentor. Another good place to start is writing a conference report.

"My first article happened when a publisher asked me to do one based on an ALA poster session that I had done. The poster session was based on a project or study that I had done in my library. My first book came out of an article I wrote, which came from a project I did in my library. There was not enough information out there on the topic in the library literature. I felt that I was helping to create the wheel. I wanted to share what I had learned with others, and hopefully, save them some time."

Consider writing with a coauthor, especially if you are new to the process. Consider whether you work better alone or with someone else. If you think a coauthor might help you, consider the following: Who is interested in the same subjects that interest you? Who is well known in this subject area? Who might add a different perspective to your book? Be sure you work well with this person, as you will have to work together for a long time, and may be invited to speak together as a result of your book. If you are coauthoring, spell out each author's duties clearly and decide how the royalties will be split. Agree on deadlines, expectations, procedures, and so on before signing the contract. If you are having contributors write for you, spell out how to write and improve pieces, give deadlines, and follow up regularly.

"I find writing alone the easiest, but I am currently in projects with others," said Kerry Smith. "So far the experience has been good. Just like group work in library school or committee work in the library, the main issue about working with others on a publication is that it can slow down the project, due to varying schedules, disagreements, etc., so bear that in mind when doing your planning."

Analyze Audience and Project

Analyze your market and your audience. What is the potential marketability of the book? Talk with other book authors, if possible, or with colleagues and friends—try to gauge the interest in a book on the topic you have chosen. Be honest so that you can talk with your publishers about the book's potential for sales.

Select a topic that can be dealt with effectively in one book. Sometimes your editors can help—for example, they may suggest that you focus on one area of your proposed topic, or they may suggest you expand the coverage of your book. Select a topic that can be dealt with in the time you have allotted to write the book.

Be sure that you have the time and motivation to spend writing a book. A book may take two to three years to write and another year or so to be published. Mentally prepare yourself for the time needed to research, write, edit, and wait for the book to be published. Prepare your family and friends for the demands that this project will make on your personal life, if you have to work on the book during your own time. At some academic libraries, you may be able to work on the book during your regular work hours. If not, find out if your workplace offers sabbatical leave, research leave, or any other support. Try to set aside a quiet place to work, whether at work or at home.

Write a Query Letter and Book Proposal

Browse books to locate publishers that might be appropriate for your book topic and that match the format you have in mind. Browse publishers' Web sites to find their focus, instructions for authors, and publication list (see table 8.1). Write a query letter to the publisher. You may write an e-mail message or mail a printed letter. Make sure that your e-mail message is written as formally and professionally as a traditional letter. In two or three sentences, describe your idea for your book and state why this book would be needed or popular. You may send a query letter first to assess interest, or you may send a book proposal along with the query letter. Sometimes the publisher will respond to your query letter asking you to send a book proposal.

When writing a book proposal, you can get the book proposal guidelines from the publisher or from the publisher's Web site. A book proposal should include a brief description of the work, a description of the audience, a list of published books on the topic, the proposed length, and a detailed outline or table of contents. If possible, include a brief description of each chapter; some publishers ask for a sample chapter. Your proposal should include writing samples (preferably a previous publication). Include a cover letter or query letter that states why the book is needed and describes qualifications to write on this topic. Include a résumé. Also, include a stamped self-addressed envelope if sending by U.S. mail. Many publishers accept these materials by e-mail. As an example, the appendix shows the book proposal written for this book. You may notice that almost everything, from topics to format to completion date, changed during the writing process.

"I am the author of three books, all published by Highsmith Press," said Ru Story-Huffman (public services librarian, Cumberland College). "I was very fortunate my first time out, as my manuscript was accepted on the second try. Since then, I have continued to publish with Highsmith, as mentioned above. I also am the technology columnist for the Big6 eNewsletter, and so far this is going well. My publishing experience has been wonderful and my publisher has been very helpful and was instrumental in getting me on an ALA program in Chicago. I think the tool that helped me the most in the process was *The Writer's Market*. I was able to locate potential publishers that matched my idea. I also found the sections on preparing a manuscript, cover letter, and general information very helpful. Since publishing my books, I have had other potential authors seek me out for tips and I usually send them to *The Writer's Market*, just as I did myself. I found that presenting yourself in a professional, positive manner was helpful, as was willingness to meet the needs of the publisher!

"Another suggestion is to obtain catalogs of potential publishers and study their lists. Try to determine what type of materials they publish, age and reading levels, etc. My publisher has a section on their Web page that details the type of manuscript they are seeking, so perhaps you can tailor your ideas to stated needs. I know my situation is not the norm, due to my very fast acceptance," Story-Hoffman concluded, "but I do know that it has been wonderful, and one I hope to continue."

Sign the Contract

It can take two to three months to hear back from publishers, but usually they will let you know what to expect within a few weeks. Often, they will respond promptly and tell you when to expect a decision about your proposal. Sometimes it may help to obtain permission to use the name of established authors or other contacts who can help you get noticed by the publisher. If you do not hear back from a publisher within a few weeks, write or call to ask politely if they received your proposal. If you still hear nothing, send your query letter to another publisher.

If offered a contract, read the contract thoroughly. Signing a contract is no guarantee of publication. Ask the potential publisher when they expect the book might be published, based on your projected submission deadline.

Write the Book

Set an achievable pace and a timeline to keep yourself on track. Keep your timeline flexible. If working with a coauthor, agree on a division of duties and deadlines. Keep in touch throughout the writing process to share ideas and monitor each other's progress.

Use file folders to break up a big project into segments. For example, you may wish to keep each chapter in a separate file folder. Set aside a specific place to file materials and work on your book. Try to find a quiet place to work and set aside a specific time to work on the book—for example, every Saturday morning, or one hour per night. Draft a schedule for writing. When writing with someone else, agreeing on deadlines can be even more important. Understand that deadlines shift, but breaking a large project up into small steps can keep you from getting overwhelmed.

Establish a consistent format in the beginning, following the publisher's guidelines. Request written guidelines if they are not provided. This will make the final editing and formatting process much easier. Use style manuals to standardize your writing. If writing with a coauthor, discuss and compare your individual writing styles. Are they compatible? You may wish to write individual chapters, then exchange chapters and edit each other's work so that the final book has one "voice."

Make backup copies of your files and keep them in a safe place. Keep a careful account of your expenses to use as a tax deduction if possible.

Edit the Book

Stay in contact with the editor assigned to you by the publishing house. Proofread the manuscript carefully for errors. If working with a coauthor, exchange drafts of what you have written so that your coauthor can read and edit your copy. Ask trusted friends or colleagues to read the drafts and provide constructive criticism. Plan to spend one or two months editing the book at the end of your writing process, if possible. By doing so, you can set the book aside for a couple weeks before rereading it; the material will seem fresher, and you will be able to catch errors you may not have seen before.

Submit the Final Manuscript

Meet deadlines or keep your editors informed of any problems. If you find that you will not be able to meet your deadline, ask for extensions early. Submit a neat manuscript, following the publisher's guidelines explicitly. Prepare your publishers for the manuscript's arrival.

Editors will send suggestions for revisions and will let you know the timeline for publication. A series of editors will correspond with you as the manuscript moves through the publication process. Stay in contact with them, and treat your editors as professionals. As with journal articles, it can take six to eighteen months for your book to appear in print. Ask your editor about the timeline for publication. The editor will also usually ask for author information and input about marketing the book.

"With my book *Teaching the Internet in Libraries*, I turned in the manuscript in June and got the copyedited manuscript back around the end of August," explained Rachel Singer Gordon. "I then made my corrections on that, sent it back to the copyeditor, received the galleys in the middle of October (laid out as the pages will be in the printed book), sent those back by the end of October, and the book itself is coming out in January. So it was something like six to seven months after I turned in the manuscript until the finished book, but they did want to get it out in time for the ALA Midwinter Meeting. ALA Editions lists a timeline somewhere on their site for the average manuscript, and I think some other library publishers do as well."

WHAT'S STOPPING YOU?

Potential authors often share several common misconceptions. In her *Serials Librarian* article, Ellen Finnie Duranceau offers helpful advice for new authors struggling to overcome these mental barriers.

"I have nothing to offer." Trust that you have a unique viewpoint. To find a good topic, collaborate with someone else, develop a case study, do an interview, or write a critical bibliographic review about some area of interest. Share ideas with others to see what interests them.

Christine DeZelar-Tiedman wrote, "My first published article was based on a paper I did in library school, so I would suggest using this as a starting point. You've already done some of the research, now expand it, update it, or test your thesis. As for submitting it for publication, don't be modest. You should have a ranked idea in your head of which journals you consider the most important—this will vary depending on the type of library you work in and the subject of your article. But go with your first choice, and then go down the list if it's rejected. As a cataloger, I submitted my first article to *LRTS*, and it was accepted. I'm glad I didn't 'think small.' That said, your state association journal and book reviews in a number of library publications are a good way to get your foot in the door."

"All good ideas have been taken." Listen at conferences, read electronic discussion lists, and sound out potential topics with others. There are always

new ideas, changes, trends, and gaps in the published literature. Be alert to new possibilities for publications.

"If my article is good enough, I won't be asked to revise it." It's unusual for any article to be published without any revision. Don't be discouraged or offended if your editor suggests revisions in your article or book.

"It is acceptable to submit an article to more than one publisher at the same time." Submit your completed article to only one publisher at a time. If you have not heard from the editor by about six weeks after submission, you can ask the editor where an article is in the approval process. If possible, send a query letter before submitting a finished article. When submitting your article, ask the editor for a projected publication date.

"If you are inspired by something enough to want to conduct research about it, or write about it, you'll know it," advised Bob Schatz. "Don't be afraid to follow your muse. Understand, though, that few things are written well the first time; good writing is good rewriting. Keep at it, and don't submit something until you are fully satisfied with it. Then accept rejection or directions for improvement if they are offered. If what you've written is worth publishing, keep working at it, or offering it for publication as long as you believe in it."

SUMMARY

- Investigate publication opportunities, including journal articles, books, book reviews, conference proceedings, etc.
- Generate ideas by brainstorming with others, reading, attending conferences, and more.
- Write a query letter to assess publisher interest in your topic.
- Write and edit the article, book, or item.
- Ask a trusted friend or colleague to read and offer suggestions.
- Send to your publisher, following their format guidelines.

RELATED READING

Publishing

Alley, Brian. *Librarian in Search of a Publisher: How to Get Published*. Phoenix, Ariz.: Oryx Press, 1986.

Axtell, James L. "Twenty-Five Reasons to Publish." *Journal of Scholarly Publishing* 29, no. 1 (October 1997): 3–20.

Catalfio, Mavis Arizzi. "Tips for Those Who Want to Write Children's Literature As Well As Catalog It (Notes From a Writer's Conferences)." *Indiana Media Journal* 11 (winter 1989): 25–7.

Chepesiuk, Ronald. "In Pursuit of the Muse: Librarians Who Write." *American Libraries* 22 (November 1991): 88–91.

Crawford, Susan Y. "Peer Review and the Evaluation of Manuscripts." *Bulletin of the Medical Library Association* 76 (January 1988): 75–7.

Cucciarre, Barbara L. "I Hate to Write, but I Love to Have Written." *Ohio Media Spectrum* 41 (fall 1989): 66–8.

Duranceau, Ellen Finnie. "Publishing Opportunities: Getting into Print or Getting Involved (Workshop Report from the 1992 NASIG Conference)." *The Serials Librarian* 23, no. 3–4 (1993): 253–6.

Gordon, Rachel Singer, ed. "Writing for Publication in the Library Environment." *Info Career Trends* 1, no. 2 (1 November 2000) <http://www.lisjobs.com/newsletter/archives.htm>. Entire issues deals with writing for publication.

Johnson, Margaret Ann. "Librarians and Contracts for Writing Professionally: The Sanity Clause." *Technicalities* 19, no. 9 (October 1999): 1, 11–13.

Kester, Norman G. "Fourteen Tips for Librarian-Authors: The Experience of a Gay Librarian-Author." *The Unabashed Librarian,* no. 100 (1996): 9–10.

Kester, Norman G. "How to Get Published." *Feliciter* 43 (May 1997): 8.

Lesesne, Teri S. "Writing the Stories Brewing Inside of Us." *Teacher Librarian* 27, no. 4 (April 2000): 60–1.

Lingle, Virginia A. "Library-Related Topics in the Non-Library Literature: Publishing Opportunities for the Health Sciences Librarian." *Medical Reference Services Quarterly* 11 (winter 1992): 23–38.

Manley, Will. "An Author's Lament (Dabbling in the Field of Library Literature)." *Wilson Library Bulletin* 66 (September 1991): 61–3.

McMillan, Gail. "Librarians As Publishers: Is the Digital Library an Electronic Publisher?" *College & Research Libraries News* 61, no. 10 (November 2000): 928–31.

Miko, Susan Kunnath. "Publish? Who Me? A School Library/Media Specialist Tells Why." *Ohio Media Spectrum* 41 (fall 1989): 61–2.

Nesbeitt, Sarah, and Rachel Singer Gordon. *The Information Professional's Guide to Career Development Online.* Medford, N.J.: Information Today, 2001. Includes a chapter on on-line publishing and a comprehensive list of publishing outlets.

Nofsinger, Mary M. and Eileen E. Brady. "Librarians and Book Publication: Overcoming Barriers." *The Reference Librarian,* no. 33 (1991): 67–76.

Palmer, Pamela R. "Librarians As Authors, Part I: Strategies for Success." *The Southeastern Librarian* 45 (spring 1995): 4–6.

———. "Librarians As Authors; Publishing Savvy." *The Southeastern Librarian* 46 (spring 1996): 6–7.

Penaskovic, Richard. "Facing Up to the Publication Gun (Writing Scholarly Articles). *Scholarly Publishing* 16 (January 1985): 136–40.

Pitts, Judy M. "Scoring Points with Professional Publication." *Arkansas Libraries* 42 (March 1985): 26–30.

Publish Your Article Outside the Library Field: A Bibliographic Guide to Non-Library and Information Science Journals with Articles on Libraries, Librarians, or Library Services. Chicago, Ill.: ALA Office for Human Resource Development and Recruitment, 2000.

Schroeder, Carol F., and Gloria G. Roberson, eds. *Guide to Publishing Opportunities for Librarians*. New York: Haworth Press, 1995.

Sellen, Betty-Carol. *Librarian/Author: A Practical Guide on How to Get Published*. New York: Neal-Schuman, 1985.

Stover, Mark. *The Librarian as Publisher* <http://www.library.ucsb.edu/untangle/stover.html> (1 March 2000).

Thomson, Ashley. "Librarian As Author: The Perils of Publishing." *Canadian Library Journal* 44 (April 1987): 93–6.

Journal Publishing

Bahr, Alice. *In Print: Publishing Opportunities for College Librarians*. Association of College & Research Libraries, 2000 <http://acrl.telusys.net/epubs/inprint.html> (1 March 2001).

DeCandido, GraceAnne Andreassi. "Not for Women Only (Writing for Professional Journals)." *Wilson Library Bulletin* 67 (June 1993): 8.

Kitta, Donna. "How to Publish in ALA Periodicals." *Ohio Media Spectrum* 38 (summer 1986): 50–7.

Logan, Karen Sue. "Writing and Publishing for Professional Journals: Ten Years of Help (1985–1995)." *The Southeastern Librarian* 45 (fall/winter 1995): 108–11.

Tee, E. R. "A Journey in Writing for Scholarly Publications." *Malaysian Journal of Library & Information Science* 4, no. 1 (July 1999): 87–94.

Book Publishing

Fischer, Russell G. "The Librarian behind the Bestseller." *American Libraries* 16 (March 1985): 158–9.

Holm, Kirsten, ed. *Writers Market 2001: 8000 Editors Who Buy What You Write*. Cincinnati, Ohio: Writer's Digest Books, 2000.

Larsen, Michael. *How to Write a Book Proposal*. Cincinnati, Ohio: Writers Digest Books, 1997.

Schuman, Patricia. "From Book Idea to Contract: Writing Reference and Professional Books." *The Reference Librarian* no. 15 (fall 1986): 155–68.

Woodbury, Marda. "On the Writing of Reference Books: Real and Ideal; In Which the Author Discourses on Motivation, Process, Publication, Reviews, and Rewards." *The Reference Librarian* no. 15 (fall 1986): 139–46.

CHAPTER 9

Conclusion

Some day you'll learn that greatness is only the seizing of opportunity—clutching with your bare hands 'til the knuckles show white.

—Mi Taylor, *National Velvet* (1944)

This book has shared advice from various information professionals for planning your career, searching for a job, gaining varied experience and education, developing your networks, improving interpersonal and leadership skills, benefiting from mentors and mentoring others, and writing for publication. Use this advice to position yourself to take advantage of opportunities that will make you happy.

BE OPEN TO OPPORTUNITY

Be available and open to new opportunities. As you volunteer for projects and make yourself known as someone who gets things done, you will have more opportunities to try new things. Be aware of the opportunities around you. Don't be afraid to volunteer for things that interest you. Take advantage of the opportunities that are offered you, especially as you are starting your career and building your reputation.

Some people plan their career objective and work toward that objective. Others—probably the majority of people—follow a more accidental career path, seizing opportunities that come along, accepting new challenges, and discovering what they enjoy and can do well.

Bob Schatz reflected, "I didn't really choose my career, though I now feel like fate was guiding me towards something that has brought a great deal of satisfaction. After I graduated from library school, I wandered through several nonlibrary jobs, partly by choice and partly by circumstance. At the suggestion of an acquaintance, I made an inquiry about library jobs at Academic Book Center, a library book jobber. While they didn't have any such leads, the company did have some needs for which I had some prior experience. There also seemed to be a good personality fit. When they offered me what was essentially a minimum wage, entry-level position, I was waiting tables and decided I had little to lose by taking it. Once inside, I was able to grow into a number of different positions, and left the organization twenty years later, having achieved the level of vice president."

LEARN TO SAY NO

Don't say "yes" to every opportunity, however. In the first years of your career, your opportunities will be more limited. You won't receive as many invitations to participate or lead projects. However, once you've established yourself as a "doer," you will quickly receive more invitations than you may be able to handle. Know your limits. Do stretch yourself—don't be afraid to try new things, but don't take on so much that you get overwhelmed or don't do things well. Balance your personal life with your professional life, so that you can create and manage a healthy, happy, satisfying, and successful career.

"A danger in equating visibility with success is that visibility may have a lot more to do with the institution than with the person," cautioned Tschera Harkness-Connell (serials coordinator, Ohio State University). "There is no question in my mind that many librarians who are extremely active nationally are heavily supported to be so by their institutions. Large, academic institutions can afford that and, in fact, the visibility is as important to the institution as it is to the person. However, if the person is competent and follows through on opportunities presented as a result of his/her profession, he/she becomes a 'success.' For example, in my own case, it is interesting to me that I have been asked to do many things since coming to OSU that I never was asked to do as a teaching academic, or even as head of technical services at a smaller institution. I am no different; I am not more competent; I just have a more visible platform from which to speak. The platform has nothing to do with me and I don't consider myself more successful because I'm here.

"On the other hand, we all know of people who spend so much time getting known that the home front suffers. Sometimes the tendency is institutionalized. Try to find a reference librarian at some academic libraries past noon on Friday! (Don't take this as a condemnation of tenure for academic librarians; I strongly support the tenure system. However, it isn't always carefully implemented.)

Harkness-Connell continued, "I think it's worth reiterating and maybe even giving examples of success stories that follow quieter routes. Teaching is one such route. We all know selfless teachers who never had a great deal of time to give to the institutionalized profession. There are also people who choose to do their jobs quietly, serve when called, but don't necessarily seek visibility. Their goal is to serve well. One of my favorite reference librarians keeps up to date on issues, attends conferences, sometimes publishes, but only gets involved in activities that directly affect his patrons. He is certainly a success in their eyes, and he is working toward the goals he considers important. As you mentioned earlier [in the book], the importance of each person defining success for him or herself is the key."

DEFINE YOUR OWN SUCCESS

Career management strategies vary wildly from person to person, just as the career you choose will be quite different from that of your fellow students, colleagues, or friends. Take control of your career. Learn what makes you happy so that you can create a career path that satisfies you.

"Sometimes you follow accidental paths instead of planned paths," mused Beverley Geer. "You create a lot of your own luck. Trust your instincts. Explore a little. Be open to change. Expect some disappointments, but be open to new opportunities.

"Serendipity surrounds us," she continued. "Learn new skills and find out what makes you happy. What makes us happy is different for everyone."

Appendix

This is the book proposal I submitted to Scarecrow Press in May 1999. As you can see, the book changed quite a bit during the writing process.

BOOK PROPOSAL: JUMP START YOUR LIBRARY CAREER

Description and Need

The first years of a librarian's career can be very overwhelming, and yet these years can be the key to creating a successful library career. Library school students and new librarians need guidance and support in order to make the most of their career. Unless one is fortunate enough to have good mentors or strong support groups, a new librarian can drift into an unsatisfying career. I would like to share advice, gathered from a variety of sources, for effectively managing a new career in librarianship.

Comparison with Other Books

Although there are several books in the business world with practical advice for creating "fast-track" careers, there is no such book in the library field. I did find a citation for a book called *Finding a Position: Strategies for Library School Graduates* (Delzell, 1982). However, finding a position is only one aspect of career management. Related books include several books on library career options and résumé writing. Some related books in the business field include:

- *Career Management Strategies for the 21st Century: The First 15 Years of Your Professional Life* (Boykin, 1999)
- *Don't Wait until You Graduate!: How to 'Jump-Start' Your Career while Still in School* (Luscher, 1998)

Audience

This book would be aimed at library school students, recent graduates, and librarians in their first ten years or so of their library career.

Authorship, Format, and Compilation Method

I would compile advice for this book by talking with successful librarians at all levels of the profession and with those in a variety of library-related professions. I would build on my own research (see "Tips for New Librarians," *C&RL News*, February 1998) and experience. As ALA New Members Round Table vice-president, I talk regularly with students, recent graduates having trouble getting their first job, newly hired librarians, and experienced librarians who are new to the association.

The format of the book would be short, easy-to-read chapters with practical, down-to-earth advice. Most sections will include tables that list specific ideas, skills, or contact information for that topic. I want to include case studies to illustrate success stories that support various topics.

Table of Contents

This tentative table of contents includes some of the topics and tips that might be included. I would estimate the total length at about 150 pages. I would like to include a general subject index at the end.

Career planning

- Assess your interests, goals, likes, dislikes, etc.
- [table: list of questions]
- Investigate various career opportunities
- [table: list of library-related careers; list of resources about career options]
- Read job ads to see what skills are required; then develop those skills
- Plan what you will learn or develop in your current position that will help you land a more ideal job next time
- Find out what you really enjoy, then look for jobs using those skills
- [table: case studies or lists of specific skills for different types of jobs?]
- Talk with people from a variety of library-related professions

Job search strategies

- Tell everyone you know that you are looking for a job (question: how to handle this when currently employed?)
- Look for job ads in journals, Web sites, phone lists, etc.
- [table: places to look for job ads]
- Write an effective résumé and cover letter [give general tips/samples]
- [table: list other books on this subject]
- Research the organization before your interview
- [table: places to research an organization]
- Prepare well for the interview
- [table: questions to expect]
- Interview the interviewer to be sure you will like the environment
- [tables: clues about your prospective environment; questions to ask in the interview; questions to ask yourself before accepting]
- Write thank you letters
- Negotiate the job offer
- Keep your résumé current (for jobs, grants, etc.)

Experience

- Get experience while in school
- Volunteer at different types of libraries or organizations to gain experience and see what environment you like
- Get diverse experience to provide variety of options and broader perspective
- Cross-train (volunteer for activities outside your normal duties)
- Gain experience you might not get at work through professional involvement
- [table, case studies: skills learned through association involvement]
- Serve on search committees to see résumés, interviews, search processes
- Serve on award committees to see résumés and selection processes
- Get public speaking experience
- Follow through on projects and deadlines to gain a good reputation
- Keep file or notebook of accomplishments

Networking

- Join professional, community, and other organizations
- [table: list organizations with descriptions/Web sites]

- Volunteer for committee involvement or for special projects
- Introduce yourself to others at conferences, meetings, etc.
- Ask colleagues to introduce you to others
- Remember names
- Volunteer for organizational activities outside your workplace
- Contact authors of articles that interest you
- Attend social functions at conferences or meetings
- Follow up on contacts

Mentoring

- Seek out mentors (formally or informally)
- Be proactive; don't be afraid to ask questions
- Mentor others; help other new librarians or students out

Interpersonal skills

- Watch how others at your workplace communicate with each other
- Learn how to get things done in your particular environments
- Learn to get along with difficult people
- [table: tips]
- Learn how best to communicate with supervisors, colleagues, customers
- [table: communication/work styles]

Leadership skills

- Chair a committee, volunteer to organize a project, etc., to gain super-visory skills
- Learn to lead from within a group (from any position)
- Develop good communication and organizational skills to get things done

Education

- Consider a second master's (especially for academic librarianship)
- Take advantage of CE opportunities
- Attend conferences and professional workshops
- [table: list places to find out about conferences and workshops]

- Develop expertise in specific knowledge areas that will help you get your dream job
- Read and research

Research and publication

- Read library publications including those outside your area of interest
- Keep a folder of your ideas
- Build on research or interests from library school
- Develop areas of research or publication expertise
- Work with others (generate ideas; coauthor articles)
- Start by writing for newsletters, etc.
- Take advantage of speaking opportunities to develop ideas, get feedback, and gain name recognition

Saying "yes"

- Be available and open to new opportunities
- As you volunteer for projects and become known as someone who can get things done, you will have more opportunities to try new things

Writing Sample

I am attaching this short article: Shontz, Priscilla K. "Tips for Surviving, and Maybe Even Enjoying, Your First ALA Conference." Accepted for publication in *American Libraries*, 1999.

I can fax or mail this article: Shontz, Priscilla K., and Jeffrey S. Bullington, "Tips for New Librarians: What to Know in the First Year of a Tenure Track Position," *C&RL News* 59 (2): 85–88, February 1998.

Projected Completion Date

I am estimating December 2000 as my completion date. I can't receive any release time from work, so I will be writing this during my free time. From June 1999 to June 2000, I will also be spending a lot of my free time carrying out duties as ALA NMRT president. I think this experience will give me a lot of ideas for this book, but I think that I would probably need several months after the end of my term.

Companion Website

LIScareer.com is a new website offering career development resources for librarians, information professionals, and students. The site was designed as a companion to this book and is loosely structured around the same topics: career planning, job hunting, experience, education, interpersonal skills, networking, mentoring, leadership, and publishing. The goal of the site, as with the book, is to help new librarians and information professionals manage a successful and satisfying career. Although the site is primarily aimed at newer librarians and students, the resources could be helpful to a librarian at any stage of his or her career. The site will include practical advice contributed by information professionals, links to online resources, and information about print resources. LIScareer.com welcomes contributed articles and suggestions. Please visit http://www.liscareer.com/ for more information.

About the Author

Priscilla K. Shontz developed an interest in career management and professional development for librarians and students through her work with the American Library Association New Members Round Table. She became actively involved in ALA NMRT in 1995 and served as president in 1999-2000. She is also active in the North American Serials Interest Group (NASIG) and other professional organizations. Priscilla has fifteen years of experience in academic, public, and special libraries. She began her library career as a student employee and earned her MSLS at the University of North Texas in 1993. She currently works as a freelance writer and Web designer. She has just launched the website LIScareer.com and edits the column "Bits and Bytes" for the journal *Serials Review.* Priscilla is working on a new book for Scarecrow Press.